CONTENTS

CLINICAL MANUAL OF SEXUAL MEDICINE
SEXUAL DYSFUNCTIONS IN MEN

I. ERECTILE DYSFUNCTION — 3

II. OTHER DYSFUNCTIONS IN MEN

INTRODUCTION

The recent introduction of **novel treatments** for erectile dysfunction (ED), particularly phospho-diesterase-5 (PDE-5) inhibitors, has **revolutionized** the management of this **common** disease. Due to the efficacy, safety and ease of administration of these agents, the number of men seeking treatment has increased dramatically. While, in the past, erectile dysfunction was a disease treated exclusively by **specialists**, it has now become a common problem seen by most **general practitioners.** The rapid developments in the treatment of ED have emphasized the importance of **continuing medical education.** The current challenges of clinical practice leave **little time** for most doctors to keep up to date with cutting edge knowledge in medicine. This **concise updated book** on the topic of sexual dysfunction in men was designed to meet this challenge.

This book presents the anatomy, physiology and clinical features of sexual dysfunction in men using a **clear, simple** and **user-friendly** format. Despite this admittedly simplified presentation, we must recognize that ED may result from **multifactorial** disease processes. The success experienced with the new PDE-5 inhibitors does not preclude the need for management of any **associated psychosocial issues** that may be concurrently present. The physician should always be attuned to the **true objective** of treatment which is not simply to induce a rigid erection, but to restore a **satisfactory sex life.**

The content of this book is based on the reports of the **2nd International Consultation on Sexual Dysfunctions.** This international multidisciplinary consultation, based on the principles of **evidenced-based medicine**, constitutes an authoritative **reference** in this field.

In addition to the most recent information on ED, the handbook provides an overview of **other sexual dysfunctions in men.**

We hope that this book, which has been meticulously prepared, will **facilitate continuing medical education** and help to **improve quality of care.**

The Editors

Further reading

• **Sexual Medicine : Part 1 - Sexual Dysfunctions in Men**
Editors: T. Lue – R. Rosen - F. Giuliano – S. Khoury – F. Montorsi ®Health Publications Ltd, 2004
Sexual Medicine : Part 2 - Sexual Dysfunctions in Women Editors: R. Basson - I. Goldstein
®Health Publications Ltd, 2004 ISBN 0-9546956-0-7 - www. congress-urology.org

• **Erectile Dysfunction Current Investigations and Management** - Ian Eardley - Krishna Sethia ®Mosby, 2003
ISBN 0-7234-3365-8 - www.elsevierhealth.com

• **Erectile Dysfunction & Related Disorders** – W. Alexander - C. Carson ®Mosby, 2003 ISBN 07234-3327-5

• **Erectile dysfunction** - T.F. Lue *N. Eng J. Med 342:1802-13, 2000*

Drawings: D. Griffiths, J-L Maniouloux **Lay-out:** S. Taieb

I. ERECTILE DYSFUNCTION

DEFINITION

Erectile dysfunction (ED) is defined as the consistent or recurrent inability of a man to attain and/or maintain a penile erection sufficient for sexual activity.

- **Consistency** is an important component of the definition of ED. Erectile difficulties must be reported to occur on a **consistent** or **recurrent** basis in order to qualify for the diagnosis of ED. A **3-months minimum** duration is generally accepted for establishment of the diagnosis. In some instances of trauma or **surgically-induced** erectile dysfunction ED (e.g. post-prostatectomy), the diagnosis may be given prior to 3 months.

The **diagnosis** of ED is primarily based on **patient's self-report**. Although the diagnosis may be supported by **objective testing** (or partner's reports), these measures cannot substitute for the patient's self-report in classifying the disorder or establishing the diagnosis.

The necessary reliance on patient's reports implies that **cultural factors** and **patient-physician communication** will be important determinants in defining and diagnosing the disorder.

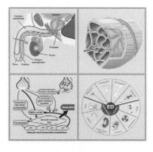

| I. BASIC CONSIDERATIONS | 4 |

| II. DIAGNOSIS | 25 |

| III. TREATMENT | 33 |

1 — The penis is composed of 3 cylindrical bodies of erectile tissue

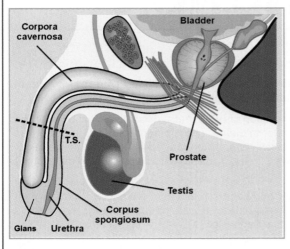

The paired **corpora cavernosa** control the rigidity/flaccidity of the penis, while the **single corpus spongiosum** regulates the diameter of the urethra for urination/ejaculation. The proximal portion of the corpora cavernosa is firmly **anchored to the pubic bone**, but the distal end is covered by the **glans penis**, a cone-shaped expansion of the corpus spongiosum.

The **corpora cavernosa** contain numerous interconnecting **vascular spaces** (sinusoids) within a **fibromuscular framework**. The **helicine arteries**, which are branches of the cavernous artery, regulate the amount of blood flow into these **endothelium-lined** vascular spaces. **Venules** draining these sinusoids form the **subtunical venous plexuses,** which traverse the tunica and empty into the **dorsal** and **cavernous veins.**

The **corpus spongiosum** is essentially a **vascular cuff** surrounding the **urethra.** The histologic appearance of the sinusoidal spaces is **similar** to that of the corpus cavernosum except that the sinusoids are generally larger.

The **tunica albuginea** is the **fibroelastic** covering of the three corpora. It consists of thick **outer longitudinal** and **inner transverse** layers with **many sublayers** in the corpus cavernosum, but only one **thin layer** in the **corpus spongiosum.** This anatomical difference provides the structural basis for the **high pressure** in the corpora cavernosa and **low pressure** in the **corpus spongiosum** during erection.

Buck's facia is a thick elastic layer surrounding the corpus spongiosum and the 2 corpora cavernosa. The remaining **superficial layers** of the penis consists of subcutaneous cellular tissue, the superficial penile fascia (Dartos fascia) and the skin.

2 — The erectile tissue consists of a lattice of vascular sinusoids surrounded by trabecular smooth muscle

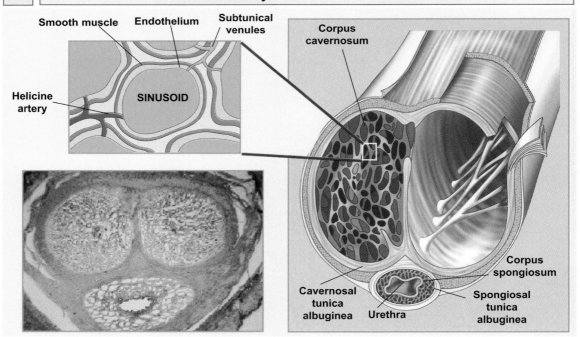

ANATOMY: Penile Arterial Supply

The arterial blood supply to the penis is primarily ensured by the **pudendal artery [8]**, a branch of the internal iliac artery. It divides into the **bulbourethral [9]**, **dorsal [10] and cavernosal [11] arteries.** *Accessory pudendal arteries* from the external iliac or obturator arteries also **contribute** to the blood supply of the penis. The **bulbourethral artery [9]** supplies the urethra and corpus spongiosum. The **cavernosal arteries [11]** enter the corpora cavernosa and continue distally in the center of the corporal bodies.

The cavernosal artery [11] gives rise to the **helicine arteries [12]**, which in turn supply the sinusoidal spaces.

The paired **dorsal penile arteries [10]** proceed down the penis along with the dorsal nerves and supply superficial structures and the **glans penis** as well as the corpora cavernosa via **circumflex arteries [13]**.

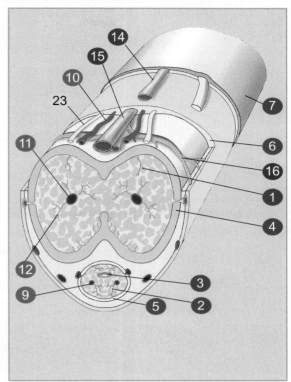

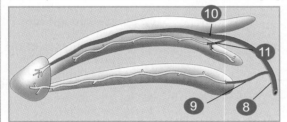

I.

PENILE STRUCTURE

01 Corpus cavernosum
02 Corpus spongiosum
03 Urethra
04 Tunica albuginea of the
    corpus cavernosum
05 Tunica albuginea of
    the corpus spongiosum
06 Buck's fascia
07 Dartos fascia

ARTERIES

08 Internal pudendal artery
09 Bulbourethral artery
10 Dorsal penile artery
11 Cavernosal artery
12 Helicine artery
13 Circumflex artery

VEINS

14 Superficial dorsal vein
15 Deep dorsal vein
16 Circumflex veins

NERVES

23 Dorsal nerve of penis

ANATOMY: Penile Venous Drainage and Erection-Related Striated Muscles

1 **The venous drainage system comprises 2 main levels: superficial and deep.**

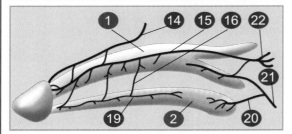

The **superficial venous system** consists of **superficial dorsal veins** [14], which drain the skin and subcutaneous tissue above the Buck's fascia.

The **deep venous system** starts with the **subtunical venules** [17] draining the sinusoids, which merge to form the **emissary veins** [18]. These veins cross the tunica albuginea and drain into the **circumflex veins** [16] which in turn join with the **deep dorsal vein** [15] beneath Buck's fascia, which ends in the **periprostatic venous plexus** [22]. The corpus spongiosum is drained by the **bulbar** [19] and **spongiosal** [20] veins, which have many channels that communicate with the corpora cavernosa. The **subtunical** and **emissary veins** are **compressed** during erection. This results in **minimal** venous drainage and **sustained erection.**

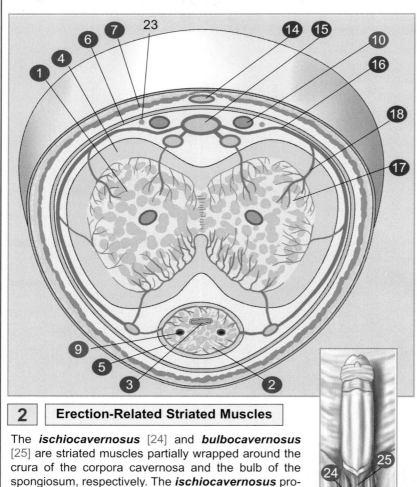

PENILE STRUCTURE
01 Corpus cavernosum
02 Corpus spongiosum
03 Urethra
04 Tunica albuginea of the corpus cavernosum
05 Tunica albuginea of the corpus spongiosum
06 Buck's fascia
07 Dartos fascia

ARTERIES
08 Internal pudendal artery
09 Bulbourethral artery
10 Dorsal penile artery
11 Cavernosal artery
12 Helicine artery
13 Circumflex artery

VEINS
14 Superficial dorsal vein
15 Deep dorsal vein
16 Circumflex veins
17 Subtunical veins
18 Emissary veins
19 Bulbar vein
20 Spongiosal vein
21 Internal pudendal vein
22 Peri-prostatic plexus

NERVES
23 Dorsal nerve of penis

MUSCLES
24 Ischiocavernosus
25 Bulbocavernosus muscle

2 **Erection-Related Striated Muscles**

The **ischiocavernosus** [24] and **bulbocavernosus** [25] are striated muscles partially wrapped around the crura of the corpora cavernosa and the bulb of the spongiosum, respectively. The **ischiocavernosus** provides the **extra rigidity** of the penis during the rigid erection phase of erection and the **bulbocavernosus** assists in the **expulsion of semen** during ejaculation.

ANATOMY: Innervation of the Penis

1 | Innervation of the penis involves both the autonomic and somatosensory nervous systems

A AUTONOMIC

Parasympathetic fibers arise from the sacral erection center (S2-S4). *Sympathetic fibers* arise in the thoracolumbar area (T12-L2) and travel in the preaortic plexus to the **hypogastric plexus.**

Preganglionic *parasympathetic* fibers from the **sacral erectile center** integrate with **sympathetic** fibers from the **hypogastric plexus** in the **pelvic plexus.**

Postsynaptic fibers travel in **cavernous nerves** to the penis. The cavernous nerve is very important for surgeons, as it travels **close to the prostate** and can be damaged during radical and transurethral **prostatectomy.** In the corpora, the nerve fibers travel in the trabeculae to directly innervate both **smooth muscle** and **endothelium**.

B SOMATOSENSORY INNERVATION

Somatosensory innervation is derived from the **dorsal nerve of the penis,** a terminal branch of the **pudendal nerve.** The sensory **afferent** information reaches the dorsal roots of the S2-S4 sacral segments from where it is transferred via anterolateral spinothalamic pathways to the integrative medial preoptic area (MPOA) in the **hypothalamus.**

However, the **pudendal nerve** also has **efferent** motor fibers that travel to the **musculature of the pelvic floor** innervating the bulbocavernosus and ischiocavernosus muscles.

During the rigid erection phase, these muscles **compress the corpora cavernosa** against the bony structures of the pelvis, thereby **increasing the intracavernosal pressure.**

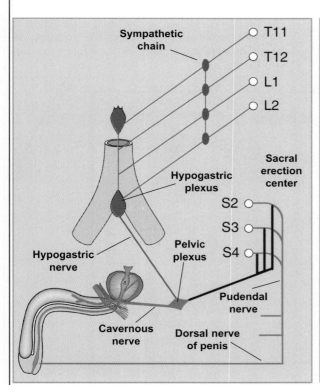

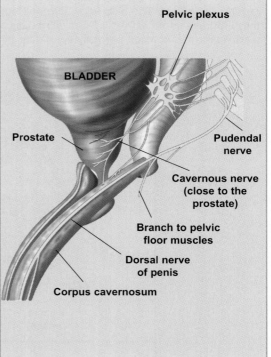

PHYSIOLOGY: Sexual Cycle in Men

1   Sexual cycle in men

Sexual stimulation induces a sexual cycle consisting of several phases of penile erection. The **main phases** of the cycle in men are as follows:

A   FLACCID PHASE

Sympathetic tone is predominant. Arterial blood flow is low and the trabecular smooth muscle is **contracted.** The sinusoids contain only a **small amount** of blood.

B   FILLING AND TUMESCENT PHASE

In response to **parasympathetic stimulation,** there is an increase of arterial inflow due to **dilatation of the arteries** (cavernosal and helicine) in the corpora and **reduction of sinus** resistance due to **relaxation of their smooth muscle fibers.** The **expanding sinusoids compress** the intracavernosal and subtunical **venous plexus** retaining the blood inside the corpora and allowing the **penis to expand** to full erection.

C   FULL ERECTION PHASE

The pressure within the corpora cavernosa is slightly **below** the systolic blood pressure and the penis is **fully expanded.** The blood flow into and out of the corpora **is minimal** (about 3-5 ml/min). This corresponds to the erection normally seen after intra-cavernous injection or after audiovisual stimulation, when the bulbocavernous reflex has not been activated by genital stimulation.

D   RIGID ERECTION PHASE

The intracavernous pressure can reach **several times the systolic pressure** in this phase due to compression of the **ischiocavernous** muscle on the base of the penis and a **complete shut down** of both arterial and venous flow. Compression of the bulb of spongiosum also enhances tumescence of the glans penis.

This phase occurs during masturbation or sexual intercourse when **direct penile stimulation** triggers the bulbocavernous reflex. If penile stimulation is interrupted or muscle fatigue occurs, the intracavernous pressure drops and the penis returns to the full erection phase.

E   DETUMESCENCE PHASE

Return of smooth muscle tone after orgasm or after cessation of sexual stimulation results in **arterial constriction,** re-opening of the **venous channels** and **detumescence.**

EJACULATION

Ejaculation is induced by **rhythmic contraction** of the ischiocavernosus and mainly the **bulbocavernosus muscle** that propels semen through the urethral lumen.

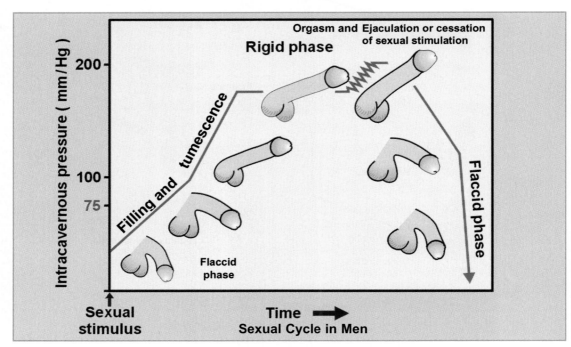

Sexual Cycle in Men

PHYSIOLOGY: Types of Erection

Schematically, there are two different types of erection: *reflexogenic* and *psychogenic*.

1   Psychogenic erection

Psychogenic erection is induced by **erotic stimuli** (visual, auditory, olfactory, tactile or imaginative), which trigger release in the brain of **neurotransmitters**, especially **dopamine, oxytocin** with also a role for **nitric oxide.** These signals are then sent to the penis by activation of the **parasympathetic** nervous system via the **Sacral Erectile Center** and the **pelvic plexus.**

The **brain** also sends **inhibitory stimuli** to the penis via the **sympathetic** system and the **status of the penis** depends on an **equilibrium** between these **proerectile** and **anti-erectile** messages. **Physiologically,** erections are **continuously inhibited** by the sympathetic nervous system, which explains why the penis remains flaccid (soft) at rest.

2   Reflexogenic erection

Reflexogenic erection is induced by **direct stimulation** of the genital organs and these stimuli are transmitted by the **dorsal nerve of the penis** to the **Sacral Erection Center.** The **efferent pathway** from the spine involves **parasympathetic fibers** via the pelvic plexus and **cavernous nerves.** The Sacral Center has connections with the **brain** which can **modulate** its action (erotic thoughts can facilitate the reflex). Reflexogenic erections may **persist** in patients with **spinal cord injury** when the **lesion** is **sufficiently high.**

3   Reflexogenic and psychogenic erectile mechanisms usually act synergistically.

Psychogenic stimuli **improve** the response to reflexogenic stimuli and **vice versa.**

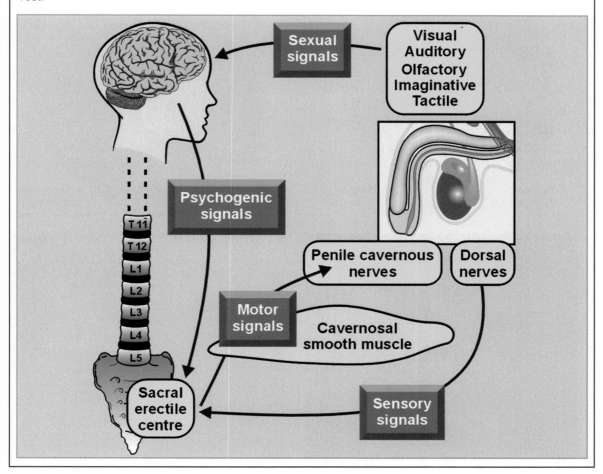

PHYSIOLOGY: Vascular Events during Erection

1 — Erection is essentially a *vascular event* depending on the balance between arterial inflow and venous outflow

2 — This hemodynamic process has three main components

1 *Increase of arterial inflow* by arterial dilatation.

2 *Smooth muscle relaxation* of the intracavernosal sinuses that fill with blood and expand.

3 *Restriction of venous outflow* by compression of the intracavernosal and subtunical venous plexus by the expanded sinuses inside the corpora cavernosa.

When *arterial inflow* in the sinuses is *low* and is balanced by the *venous outflow*, the penis remains *flaccid.* When *inflow increases* and *outflow decreases, tumescence* occurs.

In the *flaccid* state, the smooth muscle fibers of the vessels and sinusoids are *contracted.* The *emissary veins are open (as shown on electron micrograph A).* Blood can flow out *freely* from the corpora.

During *erection,* the smooth muscle fibers of the vessels and sinusoids are *relaxed.* The *helicine arteries* and sinusoids are *dilated* and engorged with blood. The *expanded sinusoids compress* the subtunical venous plexuses against the tunica albuginea *(as shown on electron micrograph B),* resulting in **markedly** *reduced venous outflow.* Blood is trapped in the corpora, inducing and maintaining erection.

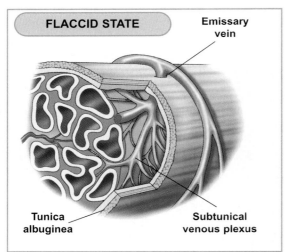

FLACCID STATE — Emissary vein

Tunica albuginea — Subtunical venous plexus

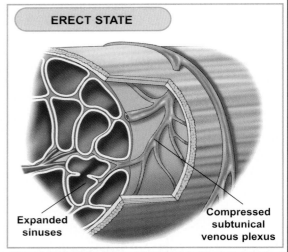

ERECT STATE

Expanded sinuses — Compressed subtunical venous plexus

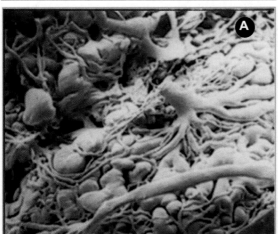

A

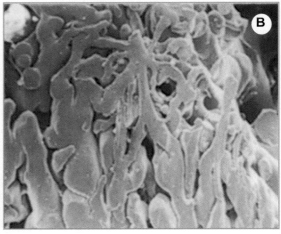

B

PHYSIOLOGY: Central Control of Erection

Neurophysiological control of erection

Erection depends on **central ①** and

② peripheral control mechanisms.

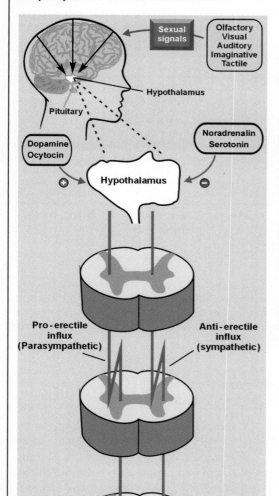

Sexual signals

Olfactory
Visual
Auditory
Imaginative
Tactile

Hypothalamus

Pituitary

Dopamine
Ocytocin

Noradrenalin
Serotonin

⊕ Hypothalamus ⊖

Pro-erectile
influx
(Parasympathetic)

Anti-erectile
influx
(sympathetic)

Cavernous
nerves

Sacral
erectile
centre

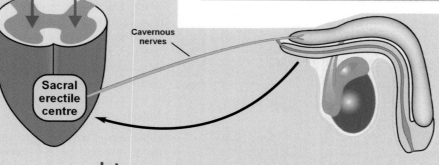

① Central control of erection

The brain is the most important sex organ. **_Erection is coordinated in the central nervous system._** Sexual stimuli are integrated in the **hypothalamus** and the message is transmitted to the penis via the **spinal cord** and **sacral erection center.**

1 — _Erotic stimuli_ originate in a variety of different centers in the **brain**

2 — The **_stimuli_** are **_processed_** and **_integrated_** in the **hypothalamus** and transformed into **_pro-erectile_** or **_anti-erectile_** messages. A number of **_neurotransmitters_** are involved in this process, mainly **dopamine** and **ocytocin** (pro-erectile) and **noradrenaline** and **serotonin** (anti-erectile)

3 — _Erections_ are **_continuously inhibited_** by basal **symptathetic** tone. **Anti-erectile messages** are mediated by noradrenaline-activated pathways and stimulate **sympathetic** outflow. **Pro-erectile messages** are mediated by dopamine-activated oxytocinergic neurons (pro-erectile) which descend in the spinal cord and stimulate **parasympathetic** outflow.

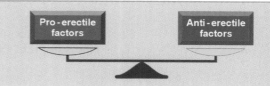

Pro-erectile factors

Anti-erectile factors

There is a constantly **_changing balance_** between the pro-erectile and anti-erectile factors. **Sexual arousal** is the result of both **increased** parasympathetic activity and **decreased** sympathetic activity.

CENTRAL ①   **PERIPHERAL** ②

❷ Peripheral control of erection depends on the balance between neuronal and local factors

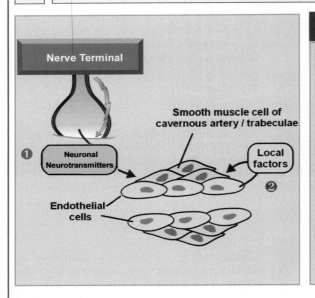

	Important factors that influence intracavernosal smooth muscle tone	
Origin	Contractile action	Relaxant action
Neuronal factors	Noradrenaline Neuropeptide Y (NPY)	**Nitric oxide** Acetyl choline Vasoactive intestinal polypeptide (VIP) Calcitonin gene related peptide (CGRP)
Local factors	Endothelin-1 Prostaglandin $F_{2\alpha}$	**Nitric oxide** Prostaglandin E_1 (PGE1)

Peripheral control of erection depends on both *neuronal* and *local factors* that ultimately influence the *vascular events* in the penis. These events depend on the *tone of smooth muscle fibers* in cavernosal arteries and sinuses. When these fibers are *contracted,* the penis is *flaccid* and *vice versa.* Smooth muscle tone is determined by the *balance* between *contractile* and *relaxing factors,* which are not only *neuronal* ❶ but can also originate *locally within* the *vascular endothelium* ❷.

1 Factors leading to smooth muscle CONTRACTION: The dominant factor is noradrenaline

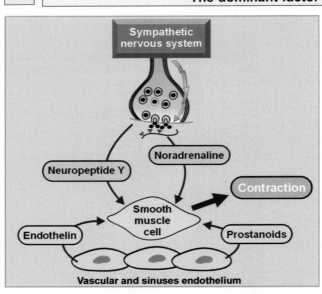

A tonic sympathetic neural input is the main mechanism leading to smooth muscle *contraction* in the penis. The *neurotransmitter of this mechanism is noradrenaline* released from sympathetic nerve endings, which binds to α-1 receptors on smooth muscle cells to induce contraction. Administration of α-*adrenoceptor blockers* into the corpora cavernosa *facilitates erection,* while α-*adrenoceptor agonists* cause *detumescence,* further confirming the role of α–adrenoceptors in the regulation of penile smooth muscle tone.

Other factors are also important: *neuropeptide Y* released by the *nerve ending* and *endothelin* and *prostanoids* (PG2α) released from *vascular endothelium.*

2 | **Factors leading to smooth muscle RELAXATION. Nitric oxide (NO) plays a central role**

Smooth muscle *relaxation* in the penis is dependent on the *parasympathetic system,* in which the most important neurotransmitter is **nitric oxide** (NO).

A Neuronal relaxing factors

Parasympathetic nerve endings release *several relaxing neurotransmitters,* mainly *acetylcholine* and *nitric oxide* (NO) .

1. Acetylcholine is the *classical* parasympathetic neurotransmitter. Acetylcholine exerts an *indirect* smooth muscle relaxing action:

a) it stimulates the *release of nitric oxide (NO) from the vascular endothelium.*

b) it reduces *stimulation of the receptors on sympathetic* endings, leading to decreased release of *noradrenaline.*

2. Nitric oxide (NO) is another neurotransmitter released by parasympathetic nerve endings.

NO is probably *the most important relaxing factor* acting on vascular and trabecular smooth muscle of the penis.

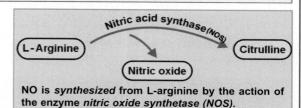

NO is *synthesized* from L-arginine by the action of the enzyme *nitric oxide synthetase (NOS).*

There are *two major sources of NO* in the penis:

* *parasympathetic* nerve endings and

* *endothelium* of corporeal blood vessels and sinuses stimulated by acetylcholine.

Clinical evidence supporting the role of NO in the induction of **erection** includes the finding that intra-cavernosal injection of *nitric oxide donors,* such as nitroprusside and linsidomine, can *produce an erection.*

3. Vasoactive Intestinal Polypeptide (VIP) and Calcitonine Gene Related Peptide (CGRP) are other substances released by parasympathetic nerve endings that contribute to cavernosal smooth muscle relaxation.

B Endothelial released factors

NO and **prostanoids such as PGE1** are relaxing factors released by the cavernosal endothelium (vascular and sinusoids)

1. NO is released by the endothelium following acetylcholine stimulation.

2. Prostanoids such as **(PGE1)** released by the endothelium also have a smooth muscle relaxing action. PGE1 induces erection when injected intracavernosally. This is the most widely used substance in intra-cavernosal therapy.

In summary, NO appears to be the most important relaxing factor in the penis. This has important therapeutic implications.

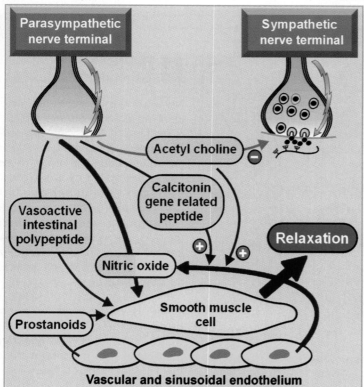

Vascular and sinusoidal endothelium

I.

PHYSIOLOGY: Intracellular Molecular Process

1 | **Neurotransmitters act on smooth muscle by changing the intracellular Ca++ concentration**

the cell that finally lead to a *change* in the intracellular calcium (Ca++) *concentration.*

Smooth muscle cells *contract* when the intracellular Ca++ concentration rises and *relax* when it falls.

Neurotransmitters, either from *neuronal* or *endothelial origin,* act by inducing a series of events in

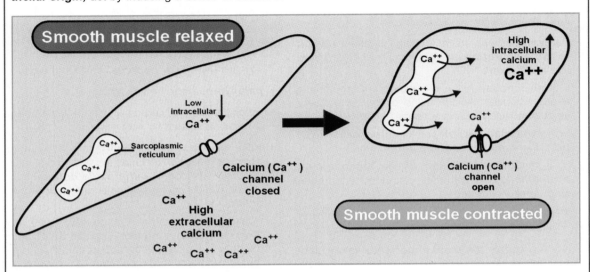

2 | **Individual neurotransmitters act via different pathways**

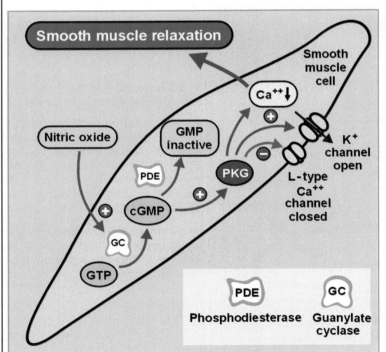

A | **Nitric oxide**

Nitric oxide is an important factor involved in penile smooth muscle-relaxation. It c*rosses the cell membrane* of the smooth muscle cell and stimulates an enzyme called *guanylate cyclase,* which then converts *guanosine triphosphate* (GTP) into *cyclic guanosine monophosphate* (cGMP), the active second messenger which *lowers intracellular calcium* resulting in smooth muscle *relaxation.*

cGMP is *inactivated* by *phosphodiesterase,* an enzyme which converts it into *inactive* guanosine monophosphate (GMP).

B   VIP and PGE1

VIP (vasoactive intestinal polypeptide) and **PGE1** act via a different pathway, by activating **adenylate cyclase,** the enzyme which converts **adenosine triphosphate** (ATP) into **cyclic adenosine monophosphate** (cAMP).

cAMP is the active second messenger which **lowers the intracellular calcium** resulting in smooth muscle **relaxation.**

cAMP is also inactivated by **phosphodiesterase (PDE)** which converts it into inactive **adenosine monophosphate** (AMP).

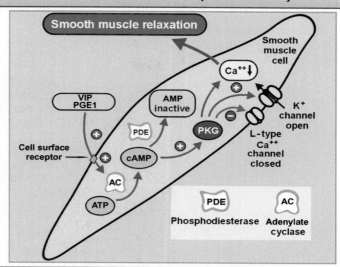

I.

Phosphodiesterase is an enzyme that plays an important role in the regulation of erectile activity

Phosphodiesterase inactivates both cGMP and cAMP responsible for smooth muscle relaxation. Drugs that **inhibit PDE** potentiate the action of cGMP and cAMP and consequently **facilitate erectile activity** in response to sexual stimulation.

There are **various types of PDE** in humans. Eleven **different types of PDEs** have been described to date. The **classification** of PDE's is based on their **structure** and **regulatory properties.** Several types of PDE also appear to be **present in penile smooth muscle.** Current evidence suggests that **PDE5** is the **most important** isoenzyme in the physiological control of normal penile erectile activity.

However, PDE5 is also found **in tissues other than the penis,** such as vascular smooth muscle and smooth muscle of the gastrointestinal tract and platelets. It is also probably present in the kidney and central nervous system.

PDE5 inhibitors are used in the treatment of ED. The **side effects** of the available drugs are due to the fact that PDE5 is also present in organs other than the penis and that these **drugs,** although highly selective for PDE5, may also **inhibit other PDE isoenzymes** present **outside the penis.** For example, inhibition of PDE6 present in the retina is responsible for the visual side effects.

PHOSPHODIESTERASES

Types	Tissue distribution
PDE1	Brain, lung, heart
PDE2	Brain, adrenal cortex, liver, goblet cells, olfactory neurons
PDE3	Smooth muscle, platelets, cardiac muscle, liver
PDE4	Very wide tissue distribution
PDE5	Smooth muscle (penis++), platelets, kidney
PDE6	Retina
PDE7	Skeletal muscle
PDE8	Testis, ovary, gastrointestinal tract
PDE9	Spleen, gastrointestinal tract, brain
PDE10	Brain, testis, thyroid
PDE11	Smooth muscle, cardiac muscle, testis

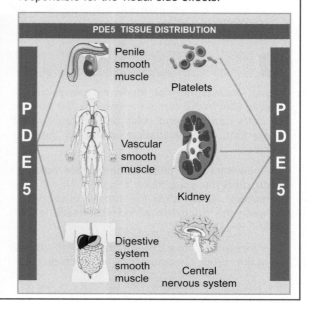

C Noradrenaline

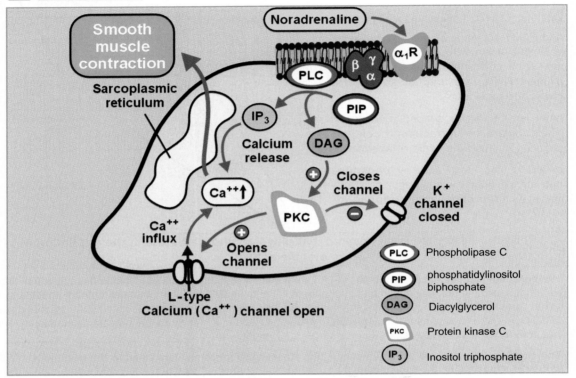

1. **Noradrenaline** acts by binding to α-1 **receptors** on the surface of smooth muscle cells.

2. It then increases the activity of a membrane-bound enzyme **phospholipase C** (PLC) which converts **phosphatidylinositol biphosphate** (PIP) to **inositol triphosphate** (IP3) and **diacylglycerol** (DAG).

3. **IP3 liberates calcium ions** from the sarcoplasmic reticulum and

4. **DAG** stimulates the enzyme **protein kinase C** (PKC) which opens the calcium channel, leading to **calcium influx** into the cell.

5. This results in a **rise in the cytoplasmic Ca++** concentration, which induces smooth muscle **contraction**.

D How is the action of smooth muscle cells coordinated ?

Nerve endings do not innervate every smooth muscle fiber in the corpora cavernosa. **So how do all cells contract and relax at the same time?** Some form of **coordination** process is therefore required.

We now know that **cells communicate between each other** by intercellular channels called **"gap junctions",** which allow the transfer of chemicals between the cytoplasm of individual cells (cAMP, cGMP, K+, Ca++).

This exchange allows **coordination** of the response of the corpus cavernosum to individual stimuli.

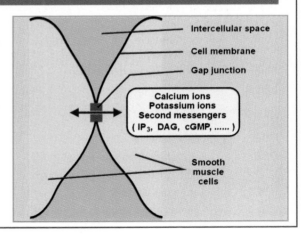

ENDOCRINE FACTORS AND ED

Testosterone is the most *important* plasma androgen. Circulating testosterone is important for *normal sexual desire* and, to a lesser extent, for *erection* (mainly nocturnal erections).

1   Testosterone (T) is secreted primarily (90-95%) by the testes, with an additional contribution from the adrenals (5-10%)

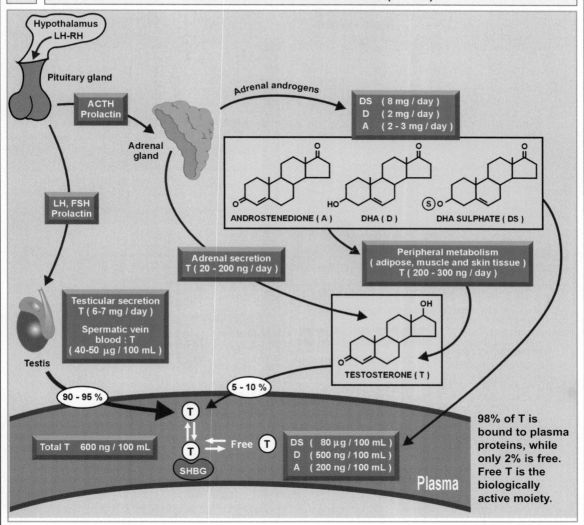

Hypothalamus
LH-RH

Pituitary gland

ACTH
Prolactin

Adrenal gland

Adrenal androgens

DS (8 mg / day)
D (2 mg / day)
A (2 - 3 mg / day)

ANDROSTENEDIONE (A)   DHA (D)   DHA SULPHATE (DS)

LH, FSH
Prolactin

Adrenal secretion
T (20 - 200 ng / day)

Peripheral metabolism
(adipose, muscle and skin tissue)
T (200 - 300 ng / day)

Testicular secretion
T (6-7 mg / day)

Spermatic vein
blood : T
(40-50 µg / 100 mL)

Testis

TESTOSTERONE (T)

90 - 95 %

5 - 10 %

Total T   600 ng / 100 mL

Free   T

DS (80 µg / 100 mL)
D (500 ng / 100 mL)
A (200 ng / 100 mL)

SHBG

Plasma

98% of T is bound to plasma proteins, while only 2% is free. Free T is the biologically active moiety.

2   Testosterone levels (total and free) tend to decrease with age

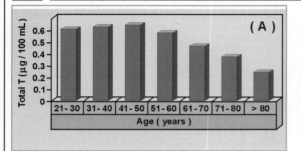

(A)

Total T (µg / 100 mL)

0.6
0.5
0.4
0.3
0.2
0.1
0

21 - 30 | 31 - 40 | 41 - 50 | 51 - 60 | 61 - 70 | 71 - 80 | > 80

Age (years)

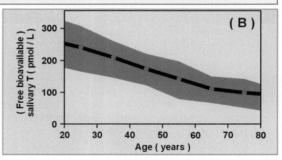

(B)

(Free bioavailable) salivary T (pmol / L)

300

200

100

0

20   30   40   50   60   70   80

Age (years)

ENDOCRINE FACTORS AND ED

2 — Testosterone acts centrally

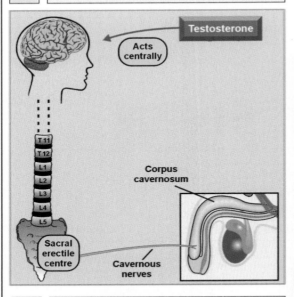

3 — Testosterone is important to maintain sexual life (androgenic action) and other important functions (anabolic action)

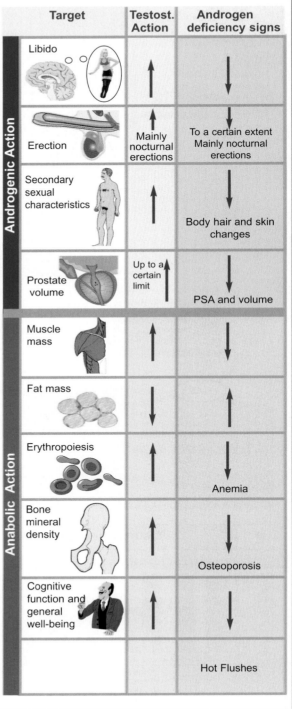

	Target	Testost. Action	Androgen deficiency signs
Androgenic Action	Libido	↑	↓
	Erection	Mainly nocturnal erections ↑	To a certain extent Mainly nocturnal erections ↓
	Secondary sexual characteristics	↑	↓ Body hair and skin changes
	Prostate volume	Up to a certain limit ↑	↓ PSA and volume
Anabolic Action	Muscle mass	↑	↓
	Fat mass	↓	↑
	Erythropoiesis	↑	↓ Anemia
	Bone mineral density	↑	↓ Osteoporosis
	Cognitive function and general well-being	↑	↓
			Hot Flushes

4 — Prolactin may influence testosterone and androgen synthesis

Mecanism of action

❶ Prolactin impairs production of GnRH in the hypothalamus leading to suppressed LH and FSH and low testosterone and spermatogenesis

❷ Direct inhibitory action on the testis

Hyperprolactinemia is a rare cause of ED. It is generally secondary to a *pituitary adenoma*. In this case, ED is accompanied by *decreased sexual interest, and spermatogenesis. Gynecomastia* is often present.

PATHOPHYSIOLOGY

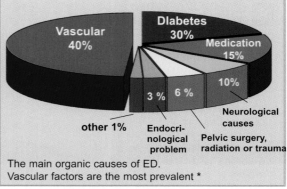

A wheel diagram with **ED** at the center, surrounded by: Psychogenic, Vasculogenic, Endocrine, Drugs, Radiotherapy, Surgical, Chronic Renal Failure, Diabetes, Aging, Neurogenic. Inner ring labels: SPECIAL CONDITIONS, IATROGENIC.

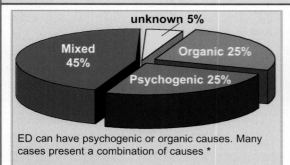

unknown 5%
Mixed 45%
Organic 25%
Psychogenic 25%

ED can have psychogenic or organic causes. Many cases present a combination of causes *

* These figures represent a rough estimate. They may vary widely with age and the population studied.

Vascular 40%
Diabetes 30%
Medication 15%
10% Neurological causes
6% Pelvic surgery, radiation or trauma
3% Endocrinological problem
other 1%

The main organic causes of ED.
Vascular factors are the most prevalent *

• Introduction

Erectile dysfunction can be due to a number of *different pathophysiological processes*.

In many patients, especially the *elderly,* more than one mechanism may be involved. In the past, it was thought that most men had a *psychogenic cause* for their ED. With a better understanding of the mechanisms leading to penile erection, we now know that many cases of ED have an *organic cause*. It has also become clear that many men present a *combination* of organic and psychogenic processes underlying their ED. This frequent *coexistence* of organic and psychogenic factors is important for the *management* of ED, which must address both facets of the disease.

PATHOPHYSIOLOGY: Vasculogenic ED

Two vascular factors are important in the onset of erection: **adequate arterial inflow** into the cavernosal arteries and an **efficient veno-occlusive mechanism** (trapping the blood inside the corpora cavernosa). **Two types of vasculogenic ED can therefore be theoretically distinguished.**

> ❶ ARTERIOGENIC **with reduced arterial inflow**

> ❷ VENOGENIC **with dysfunction of the veno-occlusive mechanism resulting in an excessive leakage of blood from the penis**

In practice, the **two mechanisms are associated** in the great majority of cases.

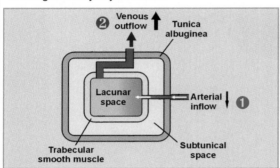

1	ARTERIOGENIC. **Reduced arterial inflow is the most frequent organic cause of ED (40-80% of all cases of organic ED)**

A Etiology

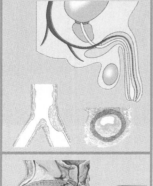

- **Arteriosclerosis** is the commonest cause of arterial disease. It is usually **diffuse**, but may be **localized** to vessels supplying the penis. Smoking, hyperlipidemia and diabetes are risk factors

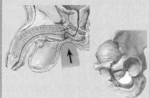

- **Traumatic injury** of the penile arteries secondary to pelvic fracture, or blunt perineal or penile trauma (much less common).

B Reduced arterial inflow leads to ED via a complex mechanism

Schematically, 2 major factors are involved.

1. The direct **negative hemodynamic** effect of reduced blood flow
2. The relative **ischemia** of the cavernosal tissue induced by reduced blood flow. Impaired tissue oxygenation induces **smooth muscle dysfunction** and **diminished expansion** of cavernosal sinusoids. This in turn prevents adequate compression of the **subtunical venules** inside the tunica albuginea with **failure** of the **veno-occlusive mechanism**. Venous leakage develops, resulting in decreased rigidity or absence of erection.

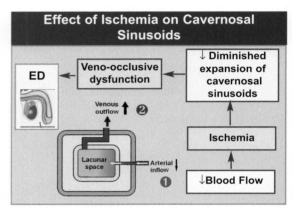

In the long run, ischemia **induces** loss of smooth muscle fibers and **fibrosis,** which further decreases the compliance of these structures and **accentuates hemodynamic dysfunction.**

In summary: although the *primum movens* of vasculogenic ED is arterial, a **secondary venous component** always develops which **accentuates** the hemodynamic dysfunction.

2	VENOGENIC. **A primary veno-occlusive defect is rare. It is generally secondary to reduced arterial blood flow**

Excessive outflow through the subtunical venules despite **adequate arterial inflow** may be another cause of ED. In this case, the **perfusion pressure** achieved cannot compensate for the **unrestricted outflow** to ensure adequate penile rigidity. **Primary veno-occlusive dysfunction** due to **anatomical** venous **abnormalities** is rare. It is generally secondary to a diminished arterial flow and ischemia. This explains the disappointing **results** of surgery to correct **venous leakage alone.**

PATHOPHYSIOLOGY: Psychogenic ED - Endocrine ED

1   Psychogenic ED

It has been clearly established that **male sexual dysfunction** is associated with **psychological disorders**. Emotional problems, anxiety or stress are significantly associated with a low level of desire, ED and premature ejaculation. There is also a clearly established **association between ED** and **depression**.

In **primary psychological erectile dysfunction,** the cause is generally found in the patient's past (social situation, sexual abuse, education, etc.) **Secondary psychological erectile dysfunction** is mainly due to specific situations, such as performance anxiety, depression and partner relationship problems.

The neurological mechanisms of this dysfunction are complex and have not been fully elucidated:

❶ Psychogenic signals may **inhibit** activation of NO-mediated parasympathetic **nerves.**

❷ **Excessive sympathetic outflow** in an anxious man may increase the constriction effect on penile smooth muscle tone and maintain penile flaccidity.

2   Endocrine ED

Endocrine abnormalities, mainly **hypogonadism** may lead to ED. **Hyperprolactinemia** and **thyroid disorders** are a rare cause of sexual dysfunction.

Hypogonadal men
have decreased **sexual interest** and desire, but do not necessarily lose **erection,** which is nevertheless **reduced** in terms of both rigidity and duration (for more details, see endocrine factors in ED).

Hyperprolactinemia

A significant **rise** in serum **prolactin** (generally a prolactin-secreting pituitary tumor) may result in **ED, reduced libido, infertility** and **galactorrhea.**

The **mechanism** by which ED occurs has not been fully elucidated. It might be due to **secondary hypogonadism**. Prolactin causes **decreased GnRH secretion** by the hypothalamus leading to decreased LH and FSH and testosterone. It also appears to interfere with peripheral testosterone metabolism.

Hypothyroidism and Hyperthyroidism

can rarely cause ED by a negative action on androgen and estrogen metabolism.

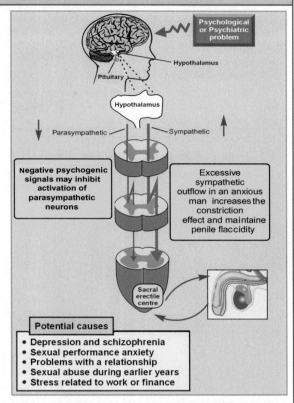

Potential causes
- Depression and schizophrenia
- Sexual performance anxiety
- Problems with a relationship
- Sexual abuse during earlier years
- Stress related to work or finance

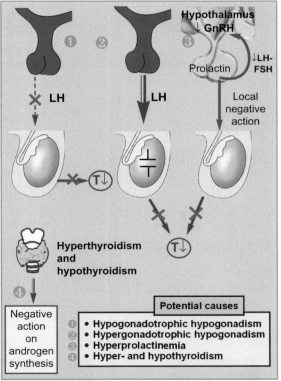

Potential causes
- ❶ Hypogonadotrophic hypogonadism
- ❷ Hypergonadotrophic hypogonadism
- ❸ Hyperprolactinemia
- ❹ Hyper- and hypothyroidism

I.

PATHOPHYSIOLOGY: Neurogenic ED

Events that disrupt *central* neural networks or the *peripheral* nerves involved in sexual functions can cause *neurogenic ED*.

10-20%

Total ED

10% to 20% of cases of ED are due to a neurogenic cause. Other causes of ED may also coexist, such as in the case of diabetes.

Erection depends on **Central ❶** and
❷ peripheral nervous control mechanisms.

Etiology

Neurogenic ED can be classified as:
❶ Supraspinal
❷ Spinal: sacral and suprasacral
❸ Peripheral

Potential causes
- **Stroke**
- **Alzheimer's disease**
- **Injuries or lesions to the spinal cord**
- **Pelvic injury, or surgery**
- **Diabetic neuropathy**
- **Multiple sclerosis**

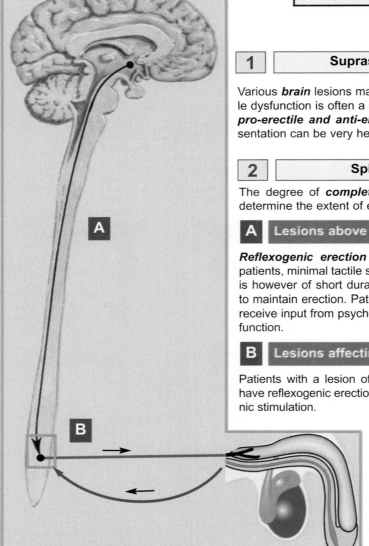

CENTRAL ❶   **PERIPHERAL ❷**

1 Supraspinal lesions

Various **brain** lesions may induce ED. In these cases, erectile dysfunction is often a symptom of the **imbalance** between **pro-erectile and anti-erectile stimuli** and the clinical presentation can be very heterogeneous.

2 Spinal lesions

The degree of **completeness** and the **level** of the lesion determine the extent of erectile dysfunction.

A Lesions above the sacral erection center

Reflexogenic erection is generally **maintained.** In these patients, minimal tactile stimulation can trigger erection, which is however of short duration requiring continuous stimulation to maintain erection. Patients with an **incomplete lesion** can receive input from psychogenic erection and maintain erectile function.

B Lesions affecting the sacral erection center

Patients with a lesion of the **sacral erection center** do not have reflexogenic erections and **do not respond** to psychogenic stimulation.

3 Peripheral lesions

Peripheral lesions can be secondary to disruption of the **sensory afferent nerves** carrying information from the penis to the central nervous system or disruption of **efferent nerves** that mediate arterial and trabecular smooth muscle dilatation.

PATHOPHYSIOLOGY: Iatrogenic ED

1   Surgical ED

Surgery can cause ED, generally by **damaging** the **nerves** and/or **arteries** that are essential for erection.

Damage to neural control: Brain and spinal surgery.

Damage to pelvic nerves: Radical pelvic surgery (bladder, prostate, rectum).

Damage to penile vasculature: Aorto-iliac surgery, surgery for priapism, Peyronie's disease, urethroplasty.

Erectile dysfunction after radical pelvic surgery

Erectile dysfunction is usually due to a **neurological lesion** of the pelvic plexus or cavernous nerves located in the postero-lateral aspect of the prostate.

The **incidence** of erectile dysfunction after radical bladder or prostate surgery, was virtually 100% in the past, but **has been improved** with the introduction of **nerve-sparing procedures**.

Maintenance of erectile capacity with these techniques varies between **35% and 70%** depending on the surgical technique, the clinical and pathological staging of the tumor and the patient's age.

Erectile function can be slowly recovered over a period of 12 to 18 months after radical pelvic surgery. **Early treatment** improves the probability **of recovering** erectile function (penile rehabilitation).

2   Drug-induced

Various kinds of drugs can induce ED. The prevalence of this **etiology is difficult to assess,** as the underlying condition treated by the drug may also cause ED (arteriosclerosis, depression, anxiety, etc). These patients are also dependent on various substances, making it very difficult to determine the **contribution of a single drug.**

The mechanism is not always clear and includes:

DRUGS and ED. Probable mechanism	
❶ Antihypertensive drugs	Decreased arterial blood flow to the penis.
❷ Hormones, H2- antagonists,	Influence testosterone levels
❸ Sedatives	Sedative effect
❹ Psychotropic drugs	Action on central nervous system

There is **little evidence** to suggest that **modifying** drug treatment can **restore** erectile function (except for hormones inducing hypogonadism).

However, it's **worth trying** in most cases, while maintaining effective treatment of the primary condition.

3   Radiotherapy

Radiotherapy to pelvic organs (prostate, bladder, rectum) can cause ED.

The pathogenesis is not clear. Radiotherapy may cause **vasculitis** which leads to **radiation damage** to small cavernosal **vessels** and **nerves**. The **incidence** of ED following radiotherapy appears to **increase over time.**

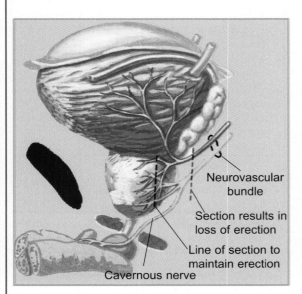

Neurovascular bundle

Section results in loss of erection

Line of section to maintain erection

Cavernous nerve

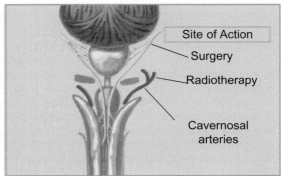

Site of Action

Surgery

Radiotherapy

Cavernosal arteries

I.

PATHOPHYSIOLOGY: Special Conditions

1 — Diabetes

A — About one-half of all diabetic men suffer from ED

Erectile dysfunction usually develops **during the course** of the disease; but can sometimes be a **presenting complaint**. The **likelihood** of ED is related to the degree of **blood glucose control**.

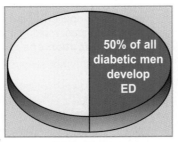

50% of all diabetic men develop ED

Diabetic men

B — The pathophysiology is multifactorial

❶ Diabetic neuropathy	❷ Diabetic arterial disease
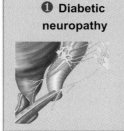	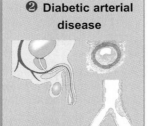

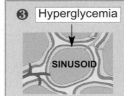

❸ Hyperglycemia

SINUSOID

Hyperglycemia has a direct action on smooth muscle cells by increasing the contractile response to noradrenaline and reducing NO-induced relaxation.

Diabetic **neuropathy** and **arterial disease have a clearly** established role in ED.

Hyperglycemia can also act **directly** on cavernosal sinus **smooth muscle**.

2 — Chronic renal failure

More than **one-half** of men with chronic renal failure treated by dialysis suffer from ED. This process is **multifactorial** and includes such factors as: hyperprolactinemia, hypertension, smooth muscle dysfunction secondary to circulating toxins, neuropathy and atherosclerosis. **Conditions** responsible for **renal failure,** such as **diabetes,** may also contribute to **ED. Transplantation** may improve ED when it is performed before the stage of irreversible damage.

3 — Aging

A — Sexual and erectile *function are generally altered with age.*

Ageing is the **most prevalent** risk factor for ED. The age related changes develop at **varying rates** in individual men.

Age-related changes in sexual function

There is a **decrease** in:

1. **Libido** and arousability

2. **Penile sensitivity** making it longer for a man to achieve erection.

3. **Rigidity** of the erection as well as the **frequency** and **duration** of **nocturnal erections.**

4. **Strength of orgasm** and the force and volume of ejaculation

5. **Frequency of sexual activity.**

B — A number of pathophysiological factors are involved and are often associated.

1. A gradual **decline** in the plasma **bioavailable testosterone** with a fall in total and free testosterone.	
2. **Atherosclerosis** and vascular changes.	
3. **Changes inside the penis** with a relative denervation of the corpora cavernosa and decreased levels of neurotransmitters including NO.	NO↓
4. A probable **imbalance** of proerectile and anti-erectile **neural tone** with an increase in sympathetic tone relative to parasympathetic tone.	
5. A **loss of cavernosal compliance** due to a loss of elasticity and smooth muscle fibers of the trabeculae.	
6. **Psychological factors** may also exacerbate any ED, especially aggravation of performance-related anxiety.	

More and more, elderly people refuse to **accept this change** of sexual function as an inevitable part of aging. With the availability of **non-invasive drugs** for the treatment of ED, an **increasing number** of elderly men may decide to seek **treatment** for their condition.

DIAGNOSTIC ASSESSMENT

I. BASIC EVALUATION

1   Medical, Psychosocial and Sexual Assessment Questionnaire

2   Physical Examination

3   Laboratory Tests

II. SELECTED OPTIONAL TESTS

1   Pharmacological Testing

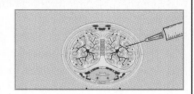

2   Color Doppler Imaging (CDI)

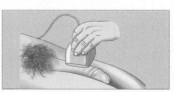

III. Diagnosis and Evaluation of ED (algorithm)

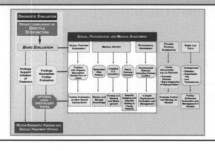

II.

DIAGNOSIS : I. Basic Evaluation

1   Medical, Psychosocial and Sexual Assessment Questionnaire

Last Name : _____ First Name _____

Occupation : _____ Date : _____

❑ Married - ❑ Married but not sexually active

❑ Single - ❑ Divorced - ❑ Widowed

A   Medical History

ILLNESS   CHECK FOR YES

Has a doctor ever diagnosed any of the following illnesses ?

❑ High blood pressure

❑ Heart disease (heart attack, chest pain with exercise or sex)

❑ Diabetes (high blood sugar)

❑ Hyperlipidemia (elevated cholesterol or triglycerides)

❑ Vascular disease (stroke, mini-stroke, blockage of arteries, aneurysms)

❑ Emotional problems (depression, anxiety or other psychiatric conditions)

❑ Hormone problems (testosterone, thyroid, steroids)

❑ Kidney disease

❑ Neurological problems (Parkinson's, multiple sclerosis, spine injury)

❑ Trauma or injury to: penis, pelvis, perineum, testes, or rectum

❑ Prostate problems (enlargement, BPH, elevated PSA, infection)

❑ Urinary problems (urgency, frequency, hesitancy, weak stream, infection)

❑ Sleep apnea (severe snoring, daytime sleepiness)

❑ Chronic fatigue or weakness

❑ Cancer (bladder, prostate, rectum or other)

❑ Radiation of the bladder, prostate or rectum

❑ Unexplained weight loss

❑ Joint pains (severe or chronic problems moving or changing positions)

❑ Sexually transmitted diseases

B   Psychosocial Assessment

IN MY PERSONAL LIFE   CHECK FOR YES

❑ I have sexual fears or inhibitions

❑ I have problems finding partners

❑ I am uncertain about my sexual identity

❑ I have been subjected to emotional or sexual abuse

❑ I have significant relationship problems with family members

❑ I have been under considerable emotional or physical stress

❑ I have a history of depression, anxiety, or emotional problems

❑ I have had a recent change in employment or finances

My sexual partner has problems with

❑ Health

❑ Sexual interest

❑ Sexual performance

❑ Sexual fears, inhibitions

❑ History of sexual abuse

DRUGS

Have you taken drugs of any kind in the last 3 months ?

1. PHARMACEUTICALS: ❑ Sedatives - ❑ For hypertension ❑ Hormones ❑ Drugs for ulcer ❑ Other

2. RECREATIONAL: ❑ Alcohol -
    ❑ Tobacco (cigarettes a day.......)
    ❑ Marijuana - ❑ Cocaine ❑ Other

C Sexual Function Assessment

Please answer the following questions about your overall sexual function in the past 3 *months or more.*

1. Are you satisfied with your sexual function ?
❑ Yes ❑ No If No, please continue.

2. How long have you been dissatisfied with your sexual function?
❑ 3 Months ❑ 6 Months ❑ 1 Year ❑ 2 Years ❑ Over

3a. The problem with your sexual function concerns: (mark one or more)
❑ 1 Problems with little or no interest in sex
❑ 2 Problems with erection
❑ 3 Problems ejaculating too early during sexual activity
❑ 4 Problems taking too long, or not being able to ejaculate or have orgasm
❑ 5 Problems with pain during sex
❑ 6 Problems with penile curvature during erection
❑ 7 Other : ....

3b. Which problem is most bothersome (circle) 1 2 3 4 5 6 7

4. What effect, if any, has your sexual problem had on your partner relationship/s ?
❑ Little or no effect ❑ Moderate effect
❑ Large effect

5. What is the most likely reasons for the sexual problem
❑ Medical illness or surgery
❑ Prescription Medications
❑ Stress or relationship problems
❑ Don't know

6. AROUSAL/PERFORMANCE - a) Chronology
• When was the last time you had a satisfactory erection? _____
• Was the onset of your problem
  ❑ gradual or ❑ sudden?
• When was your last normal erection? _____

AROUSAL/PERFORMANCE - b) Quantify
CHECK FOR YES
❑ Do you have morning or night time erections?
❑ On a scale of 1 to 5 rate your rigidity during sex?
  1 2 3 4 5
❑ With sexual stimulation can you initiate an erection?
❑ With sexual stimualtion can you maintain an erection?

AROUSAL/PERFORMANCE c) Qualify CHECK FOR YES
❑ Is your erectile dysfunction partner or situational specific?
❑ Do you lose erection before penetration, or before climax?
❑ Do you have to concentrate to maintain an erection?
❑ Is there a significant bend in your penis?
❑ Do you have pain with erection?
❑ Are there any sexual positions that are difficult for you?

7. LIBIDO / INTEREST
❑ Do you still look forward to sex?
❑ Do you still enjoy sexual activity?
❑ Do you fantasize about sex?
❑ Do you have sexual dreams?
❑ How easily are you sexually aroused (turned on)?
❑ How strong is your sex drive?

8. EJACULATION / ORGASM / SATISFACTION
❑ Are you able to ejaculate when you have sex?
❑ Are you able to ejaculate when you masturbate?
❑ If you have a problem with ejaculating, is it:
  ❑ You ejaculate before you want to?
  ❑ You ejaculate before your partner wants you to?
  ❑ You take too long to ejaculate?
  ❑ You feel like nothing comes out?
❑ Do you have pain with ejaculation?
❑ Do you see blood in your ejaculation?
❑ Do you have difficulty reaching orgasm?
❑ Is your orgasm satisfying?
❑ What percentage of sexual attempts are satisfactory to your partner?_____

9. PREVIOUS CONSULTATIONS
❑ Have you consulted a physician or counselor for your sexual problems ?
❑ If yes, what type of physician or counselor have you consulted (check all that apply) :
❑ General practitioner - ❑ Urologist
❑ Other specialist - ❑ Counselor or psychologist
❑ Are you taking any medication or receiving medical treatment for the problem?
• If yes, what medical or other non-medical treatments are you using ? _____
• How effective has the treatment been ?
  ❑ Not at all effective - ❑ Somewhat effective
  ❑ Very effective

II.

2   Physical Examination

Should be carried out in **each patient** presenting for sexual dysfunction looking in particular for signs of **conditions** known to be **associated with ED**, and **influencing** the final **management.**

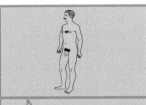

❶ **General appearance** and **secondary sexual characteristics** in search of hypogonadism, or feminization.

❷ **Cardiovascular**, blood pressure and peripheral pulses

❸ **Genitalia.** Size and shape of the penis (check for fibrotic plaque suggestive of Peyronie's disease). Abnormalities of the prepuce, testicular size.

❹**Digital rectal examination** (in patients over 50) to evaluate the prostate and anal sphincter tone.

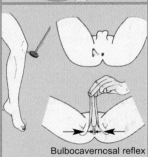

Bulbocavernosal reflex

❺ **Oriented Neurological exam**. Assessment of lower limb sensitivity. Perineal and anal tone and sensation. **Penile sensation.** Bulbocavernosal reflex (compression of the glans triggers anal contraction).

3   Laboratory Tests

The physician must **tailor** the laboratory work-up based on the patient's complaints and **risk factors** (Diabetes, hyperlipidemia...). **Testosterone** (Total and bioavailable) should also be measured between 8-10 am.

if T low
↓
T (confirmation)
LH
FSH
Prolactin

A variety of **special investigations** are available to provide more detailed understanding of the erectile process. However the **majority of these tests** are of **limited value** in managing the individual patient especially with the introduction of oral treatment. They should be *reserved* for **selected patients**. Two of these tests used in clinical practice are described below.

| 1. Pharmacological Testing | 2. Color Doppler Imaging |

Other tests **non specific to ED** itself are also needed to evaluate **etiological factors** (Diabetes, hormonal) and potential **contraindications** to direct therapies (unstable cardiac disease).

1   Pharmacological Testing

Intracavernous injection of a vasodilator is used as a test to differentiate **vasculogenic** from **non-vasculogenic ED. If after injection** of the intracavernosal drug (generally PGE1) an **erection is achieved** within 10 minutes, venous and arterial insufficiency are **unlikely.** Men with moderate to severe venous insufficiency would have difficulty achieving a pharmacological erection. **If a full erection is not seen** or if the erection lasts only a short time, the patient is allowed to **stimulate himself** in an attempt to improve the response. Again if a good-quality sustained erection is achieved, then severe arterial or venous insufficiency is unlikely. **Failure after stimulation** is considered to be a good indicator of the presence of **vasculogenic ED.** Caution: Patient with severe anxiety or needle phobia may not respond to this test.

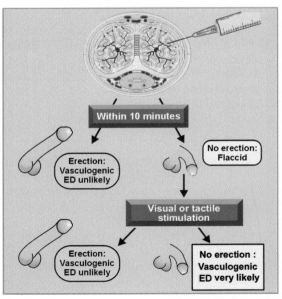

Within 10 minutes

Erection: Vasculogenic ED unlikely

No erection: Flaccid

Visual or tactile stimulation

Erection: Vasculogenic ED unlikely

No erection: Vasculogenic ED very likely

2 | Color Doppler Imaging (CDI)

Penile blood flow study by color duplex ultrasound *after intracavernosal injection* with a vasoactive agent may provide *further information* over injection alone in identifying *vascular ED.* This is a *good screening test* to select patients who need more invasive testing or treatment.

A | TECHNIQUE

After intracavernosal injection of a vasoactive agent (PGE 1) the penis can be scanned by a dorsal or ventral approach at the base, with the probe held transversely or in an oblique longitudinal position. The *velocity of blood* in the cavernosal artery during *systolic* and *diastolic* phases is recorded within 5 minutes of injection and repeated frequently until a stepwise evaluation of the *entire erectile cycle* has been accomplished.

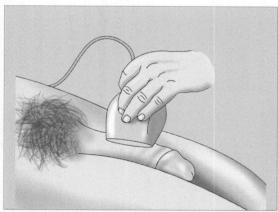

B | RESULTS

A low resistance tissue bed, as in the relaxed cavernosal sinusoids in the early phase of erection, will allow forward flow with high diastolic velocity. *A high resistance* vascular bed, such as the engorged sinusoids of the erect penis or tonic cavernosal sinusoids in the flaccid penis, would only allow flow during the high-pressure systolic portion of the cardiac cycle. During diastole, the pressure would be insufficient to overcome the peripheral vascular resistance and the diastolic flow would be low or nil.

Measurements made by CDI are *subject to variations* in the same patient studied on two occasions (about 25%). *This affects the reliability* of the test for diagnosis and monitoring of patients. However, Doppler is a good technique to make the differential diagnosis of no flow and high flow priapism.

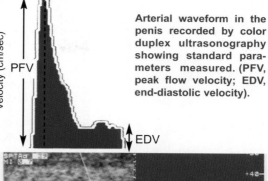

Arterial waveform in the penis recorded by color duplex ultrasonography showing standard parameters measured. (PFV, peak flow velocity; EDV, end-diastolic velocity).

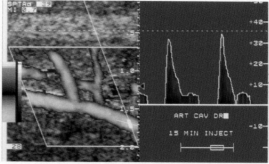

Fig. 1 Normal vascular response. Peak flow velocity (PFV) >35 cm/s, End-diastolic velocity (EDV) nil

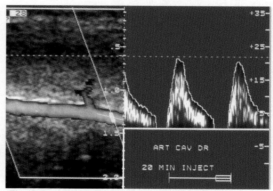

Fig. 2 Arterial insufficiency : PFV <25cm/s

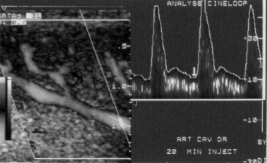

Fig. 3. Veno-occlusive dysfunction: 20 minutes after intracavernous injection and sexual stimulation. PFV >35cm/sec and EDV>5 cm/sec
(courtesy of Dr Tordjman - Paris)

II.

III. Diagnosis and Evaluation of ED (algorithm)

All men with ED should be *evaluated* by a health care professional with a sensitivity toward cultural, ethnic and religious factors. A *multidisciplinary approach* may be required in *some cases.*

The *diagnostic tests* utilized in the assessment of the patient with ED may be stratified as:

- **Basic evaluation:** an assessment *necessary in all patients* (See Diagnostic Algorithm). **All patients with ED should receive a sexual, medical and psychosocial history, physical examination and focused laboratory tests.**

  - *Optional tests:* tests of proven value in the evaluation of *specific patient profiles,* with use left to the *clinical judgment* of the treating physician in general practice.
  - *Specialized tests:* tests of value in select patient profiles in *specialized settings.*

The rationale for testing and potential impact of a positive test should be explained to the patient (e.g. an abnormal fasting glucose result may lead to the diagnosis of diabetes).

Basic Evaluation

1 Sexual, medical and psychosocial assessment

These are the most important elements in the basic evaluation of ED. This *history* should be obtained *in all patients* presenting with complaints consistent with ED.

In the evaluation of ED, particular attention should be paid to:
- Patient expectations.
- Partner involvement

When *psychosocial assessment* reveals the presence of *significant psychological distress or partner conflict,* further evaluation and management may be necessary either prior to, or in conjunction with treatment of ED (See Diagnostic Algorithm).

Referral to an appropriate *mental health professional* may be indicated in *some cases.*

2 Focused physical examination

3 Basic laboratory tests

The physician must tailor the laboratory work-up based on the patient's complaints and risk factors. Testosterone (total + bioavailable or free) should be measured.

2 Optional and/or Specialized Diagnostic Testing

As indicated in the Diagnostic Algorithm, these tests are designed to further *evaluate specific etiological conditions* or factors, or to evaluate *potential contraindications* to direct therapies for ED (e.g. unstable cardiac disease). Patients should be *fully informed* as to the rationale for these tests and the results of testing should be *reviewed with the patient.*

While the *majority* of patients with ED can be *managed* within the *primary care setting* by a physician educated in male sexual dysfunction, specific circumstances may dictate the need for *referral* for specialized testing and/or treatment

CONCLUSION

The *first step* in the management of the patient with ED is to facilitate the patient's and partner's (if available) *understanding of the condition,* the results of the *diagnostic assessment* and to identify the patient's and partner's *needs, expectations, priorities and preferences.*

The *degree to which patients and partners are bothered or distressed* by the condition is especially important to assess as this influences treatment indications and modalities.

The *identification and recognition of medical and psychological factors associated with ED* in the individual patient should be emphasized.

ALGORITHM FOR DIAGNOSTIC EVALUATION OF ED

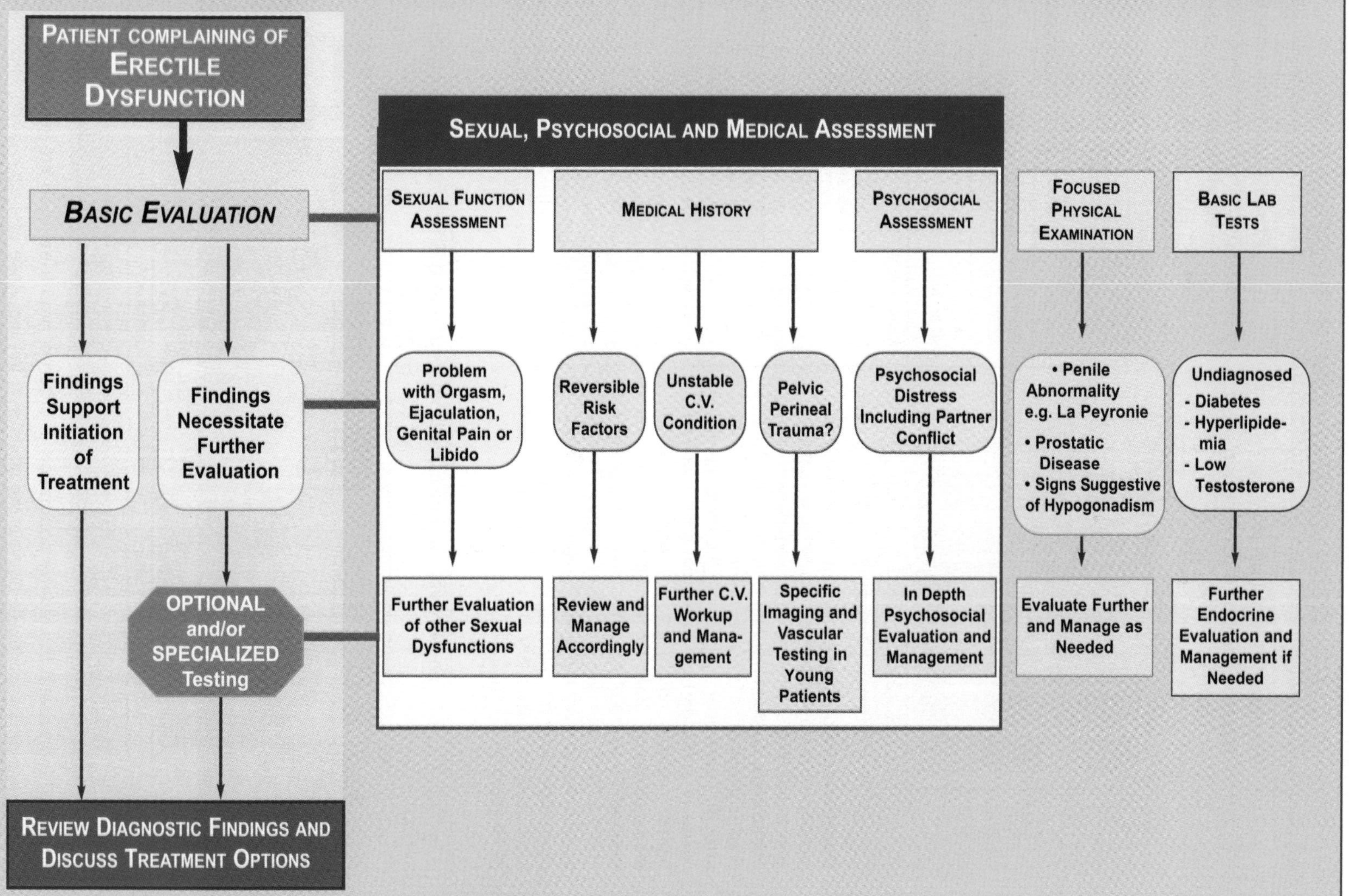

II.

PATIENT COMPLAINING OF ERECTILE DYSFUNCTION

→ **BASIC EVALUATION**

- → Findings Support Initiation of Treatment
- → Findings Necessitate Further Evaluation → OPTIONAL and/or SPECIALIZED Testing

→ REVIEW DIAGNOSTIC FINDINGS AND DISCUSS TREATMENT OPTIONS

SEXUAL, PSYCHOSOCIAL AND MEDICAL ASSESSMENT

SEXUAL FUNCTION ASSESSMENT
→ Problem with Orgasm, Ejaculation, Genital Pain or Libido
→ Further Evaluation of other Sexual Dysfunctions

MEDICAL HISTORY
- → Reversible Risk Factors → Review and Manage Accordingly
- → Unstable C.V. Condition → Further C.V. Workup and Management
- → Pelvic Perineal Trauma? → Specific Imaging and Vascular Testing in Young Patients

PSYCHOSOCIAL ASSESSMENT
→ Psychosocial Distress Including Partner Conflict
→ In Depth Psychosocial Evaluation and Management

FOCUSED PHYSICAL EXAMINATION
→ • Penile Abnormality e.g. La Peyronie
• Prostatic Disease
• Signs Suggestive of Hypogonadism
→ Evaluate Further and Manage as Needed

BASIC LAB TESTS
→ Undiagnosed
- Diabetes
- Hyperlipidemia
- Low Testosterone
→ Further Endocrine Evaluation and Management if Needed

ERECTILE DYSFUNCTION: PREVALENCE

1 Erectile dysfunction (ED) is widespread and the prevalence increases with aging

2 Prevalence rates may vary depending upon the conditions and standards of the epidemiological study

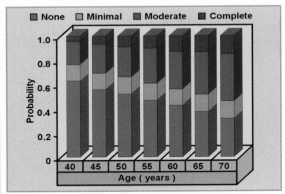

Questionnaire and survey studies in both community and clinic-based samples, covering a variety of sexual activities and functions, have provided some *descriptive epidemiological data* to suggest that erectile dysfunction is *a prevalent* disorder in *men after 40 years* of age. Accepting the profound difficulties in acquiring hard data from such questionnaires, studies such as the early classical *Massachusetts Male Aging Study* of men between *40-70 years* of age, indicated a probability of about *52%* of men revealing some degree of erectile dysfunction, from *minimal,* through *moderate* to *complete,* with the probability of complete ED, increasing from about *5%* at the age of *50,* to *15%* at *70 years*.

References	Age decades	Prevalence rate
Kongkanand et al, 2000	50-59	22
	60-70	49
Braun et al 2001	50-59	16
	60-69	34
	70-76	53
Meuleman et al, 2001	50-59	9
	60-69	22
	70-79	38
Blanker et al 2001	50-54	3
	55-59	5
	60-64	11
	65-69	19
	70-78	26
Martin-Morales et al, 2001	50-59	8
	60-70	21
Green 2001	55-60	7
	61-65	13
	66-70	22

Other more *recent studies* have produced data showing some *differences* of prevalence, mainly due to the use of different screening questionnaires and intensity scales. This highlights the need to *standardize* screening procedures by using a unified internationally accepted questionnaire and definitions of the intensity of sexual dysfunction.

3 The Prevalence of ED will increase in the future, due to aging of the population

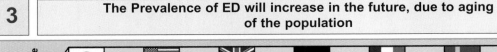
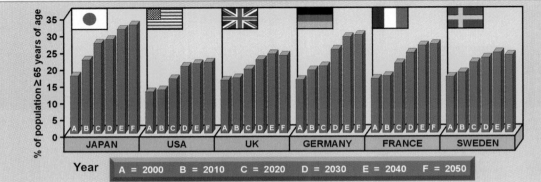

Projected increase in the elderly population in different countries up to the year 2050.

Current data on the worldwide aging of the planet's population clearly suggest a potential increase in the incidence of erectile dysfunction over the next few decades.

TREATMENT

PHARMACOLOGICAL THERAPY

1   **Centrally acting drugs (Brain)**

Apomorphine (oral)

Yohimbine (oral)

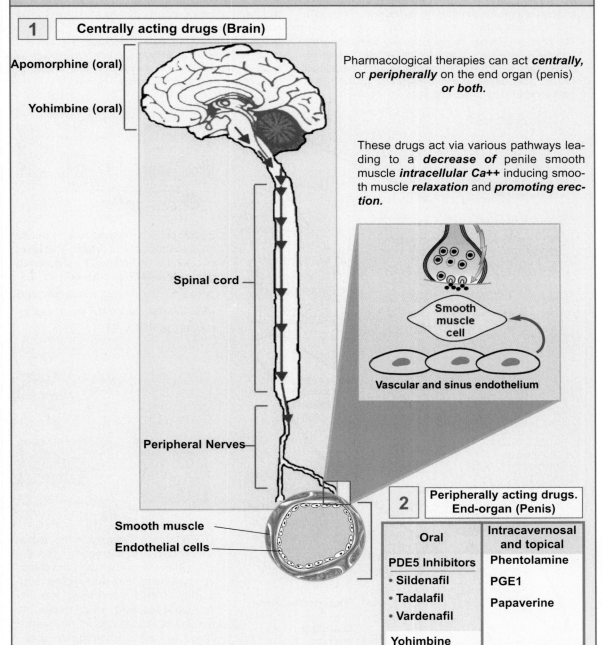

Pharmacological therapies can act **centrally,** or **peripherally** on the end organ (penis) **or both.**

These drugs act via various pathways leading to a **decrease of** penile smooth muscle **intracellular Ca++** inducing smooth muscle **relaxation** and **promoting erection.**

Smooth muscle cell

Vascular and sinus endothelium

Spinal cord

Peripheral Nerves

Smooth muscle

Endothelial cells

2   **Peripherally acting drugs. End-organ (Penis)**

Oral	Intracavernosal and topical
PDE5 Inhibitors	Phentolamine
• Sildenafil	PGE1
• Tadalafil	Papaverine
• Vardenafil	
Yohimbine	

III.

ORAL THERAPY: PDE5 inhibitors

1 **PDE5-inhibitors are the reference class in ED oral therapy. They enhance penile smooth muscle relaxation and penile erection in response to sexual stimulation**

Erection depends on *relaxation* of the penile *cavernosal smooth muscle.* Although the control mechanism is complex, *nitric oxide (NO)* is the *most important* chemical *mediator* of penile smooth muscle relaxation.

NO is *released* directly from *parasympathetic* nerve endings and from *vascular endothelium* in response to sexual stimulation.

NO *acts* on smooth muscle cells by stimulating the enzyme *guanylate cyclase* to convert *guanosine triphosphate* (GTP) into the active second messenger *cyclic guanosine monophosphate* (cGMP) that induces smooth muscle relaxation.

cGMP is *broken down* by an enzyme *phosphodiesterase* (PDE5) into inactive GMP.

The *cGMP concentration* in the smooth muscle cell is the result of a *balance* between the intensity of the *NO stimulus* and the rate of *cGMP breakdown* by PDE5 which is why PDE5, plays an *important role* in the regulation of penile activity and has important *repercussions* for the *treatment* of ED.

Drugs which *inhibit PDE5* increase the action of cGMP and thereby *enhance* penile cavernous and vascular smooth muscle *relaxation* and erection in response to *sexual stimulation.*

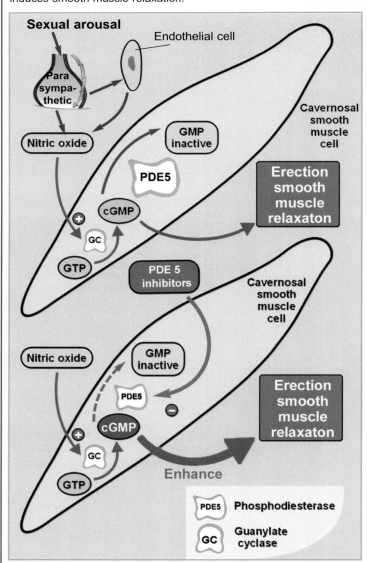

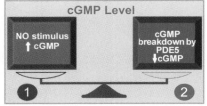

cGMP plays a *central role* in penile smooth muscle *relaxation*. The *level* of cGMP is determined by a *balance* between *cGMP production* in response to the NO stimulus **①** and *deactivation of cGMP* by phosphodiesterase PDE5 **②**

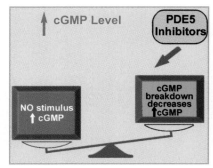

PDE5 inhibitors *decrease* the degradation of cGMP, *increasing* thereby the cGMP concentration in the corpora cavernosa and the vessels supplying it. This *increases* smooth muscle *relaxation* which dilates the sinusoids resulting in increased blood flow and *enhancing erection.*

ORAL THERAPY: PDE5 inhibitors

2	**There are various types of PDE in humans.** **PDE5 is the most important subtype for penile smooth muscle activity**

PDE5 SITES OF ACTION

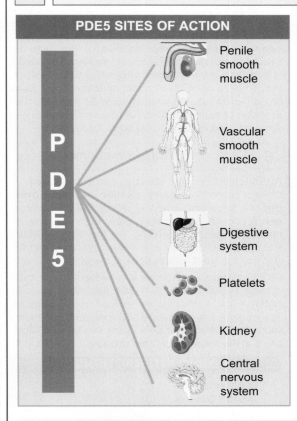

Penile smooth muscle

Vascular smooth muscle

Digestive system

Platelets

Kidney

Central nervous system

There are various types of PDE in humans. *11 different families* of PDE have been described to date. *The classification of PDE* is based on their *structure* and *regulatory* properties.

Several types of PDE are present in *penile smooth muscle*. Current evidence suggests that *PDE5* is the isoenzyme with the *most important* physiological role in the control of normal penile erectile activity.

However, PDE5 is found in *tissues other than the penis,* such as vascular smooth muscle, smooth muscle of the gastrointestinal tract and in platelets. It is probably also present in the kidney and central nervous system.

PDE5 inhibitors are used in the treatment of ED.

The *side effects* of the available PDE5 inhibitors are due to the following:

1. PDE5 isoenzyme is present in *organs other than the penis*. Side effects are caused by PDE5 inhibition in smooth muscle tissue outside the penis mainly vascular and gastrointestinal (such as headache, facial flushing, nasal stuffiness and dyspepsia).

2. The drugs may also *inhibit other PDE isoenzymes* present in organs other than the penis. For example, inhibition of PDE6 present in the retina is responsible for visual side effects.

PHOSPHODIESTERASES

Family	Tissue distribution
PDE1	Brain, lung, heart
PDE2	Brain, adrenal cortex, liver, goblet cells, olfactory neurons
PDE3	Smooth muscle, platelets, cardiac muscle, liver
PDE4	Very wide tissue distribution
PDE5	Smooth muscle (penis++), platelets, kidney
PDE6	Retina
PDE7	Skeletal muscle
PDE8	Testis, ovary, gastrointestinal tract
PDE9	Spleen, gastrointestinal tract, brain
PDE10	Brain, testis, thyroid
PDE11	Smooth muscle, cardiac muscle, testis

III.

ORAL THERAPY: PDE5 inhibitors

3

Three members of the PDE5 inhibitors class are currently available for clinical use: sildenafil, vardenafil and tadalafil

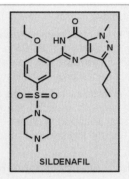

SILDENAFIL

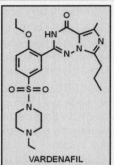

VARDENAFIL

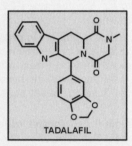

TADALAFIL

4

PDE5-inhibitors are associated with the broadest efficacy and tolerability of oral ED therapies

PDE5-inhibitors are therefore considered to be the *reference class* for oral treatment.

PDE5-inhibitors are *effective* and *well tolerated*, as demonstrated by *controlled clinical trials* and clinical practice experience. There is a *high level of evidence* for the *efficacy* of all three drugs in general ED.

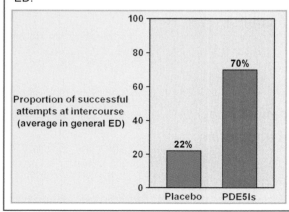

Proportion of successful attempts at intercourse (average in general ED)

- Placebo: 22%
- PDE5Is: 70%

5 **Action of PDE5-Inhibitors**

The class is registered for *on-demand use.* The clinical action of PDE5-inhibitors may be detected after the *first intake.* However, patients must be taught how to *optimally use the drug* because of the need for *sexual stimulation* and adequate *dosing.* The results of treatment are therefore improved by patient education. There is variability of *onset of action* for the three drugs (which may be at least 15 to 30 minutes). The *duration of action* is about five hours for sildenafil and vardenafil and up to 24 to 36 hours for tadalafil.

6 **Drug interactions**

PDE5-inhibitors are **strictly contraindicated** in patients receiving *organic nitrates* and *nitric oxide donors.* In patient receiving concomitally *an α-blocker* recommendation may vary from *caution* to *contraindication* depending on the PDE5-inhibitor and the α-blocker to be used. Physicians must carefully follow the *label instructions* of these drugs.

PDE5-inhibitors undergo hepatic metabolism via cytochrome P450CYP3A4. *CYP3A4 inhibitors* such as erythromycin, ketoconazole, and protease inhibitors, can increase the levels of PDE5-inhibitors. In patients taking these drugs, consider administering PDE5-inhibitors at the *lowest available dosage.*

DRUG INTERACTIONS	
Organic nitrate Nitrate Donors	**Absolute Contraindication**
α-blockers	Caution or contraindication depending on the PDE5 inhibitor and the α-blocker to be used *
CYP 3A4 Inhibitors • Erythromycin, • Ketoconazole, • Protease inhibitors	Give the lowest possible dose of PDE5-inhibitors

* Physicians must carefully follow the label instructions of the drugs to be used

7 **Side effects are usually mild**

These three PDE5-inhibitors are associated with *class-related side effects* including headache, dyspepsia, facial flushing, and nasal stuffiness. *Other side effects,* such as abnormal vision (due to PDE6 inhibition), myalgia and back pain, may vary according to the specific compound used. These side effects are predominantly *mild to moderate.*

ORAL TREATMENT: Apomorphine, Yohimbine

1 | **Apomorphine acts centrally on the D2 dopaminergic receptors in the hypothalamus**

It is available as a sublingual preparation (Apomorphine SL) for the treatment of men with ED.

Its **onset of action** is less than 20 minutes.

Treatment should be started at a **dosage** of 2 mg that can be increased to 3 mg if necessary and if well tolerated.

Clinically, apomorphine is associated with **modest efficacy** and **good tolerability** in **mild ED.**

Side effects include mild-to-moderate nausea, dizziness, yawning and rare bradycardia/syncope (vasovagal) syndrome.

Patients should be advised not to drive for **two hours** after taking apomorphine because of the risk of **dizziness** and they should **avoid alcohol.** Apomorphine should be administered cautiously to men with a history of **postural hypotension** and the patient should be advised to lie down if he experiences prodromal symptoms.

2 | **Yohimbine is an α2-adrenergic blocker that acts both centrally and peripherally**

There is a **low level** of evidence for the efficacy of yohimbine in ED. The usual **dosage** is 15 to 30 mg per day in divided doses.

Side effects include palpitations, urinary frequency, nausea, indigestion, headache and transient hypertension.

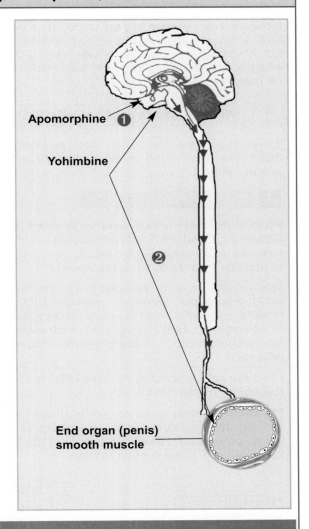

Apomorphine **❶**

Yohimbine

❷

End organ (penis) smooth muscle

CONCLUSION ON ORAL DRUGS

The advantages of oral drug therapies include broad patient acceptance, ease of administration and relative efficacy.

The disadvantages include specific contraindications, such as the concomitant use of nitrates with respect to PDE5-inhibitors, and the relative cost.

Discontinuation rates in clinical trials are low. In clinical practice, discontinuation rates may be higher for a number of reasons, including **inadequate patient education** and follow-up, **cost** and possibly **psychological factors**.

Good patient information about the optimal ways of taking treatment (dosage, need for sexual stimulation, etc.) is important for the success of treatment and patient satisfaction.

The introduction of oral **therapy** for ED has been a **revolution** in the **management** of this disease. **ED nevertheless remains** a **multifaceted process** and introduction of a rapid and easy **pharmacological solution** does not eliminate the need for management of the **associated psychological issues.** We should always remember that the **objective** of treatment **is not just to induce a rigid erection,** but to restore a **satisfactory sex life.**

III.

INTRACORPOREAL PHARMACOLOGICAL THERAPY

Intracorporeal injection therapy introduced in the early 1980s was a *milestone* in the treatment of ED. It was the first time that a *safe* and *highly effective* pharmacologic treatment was *available for* many men with ED

1 | What drugs are used for injection?

Three drugs have been used most frequently: **PGE1**, (the most widely used), *papaverine* and *phentolamine.*

A | Prostaglandin E1 (PGE1)

PGE1 in the *most widely used* single agent for intracorporeal injection. It acts primarily via specific receptors on the surface of the smooth muscle cell to stimulate the enzyme *adenylate cyclase.*

This enzyme converts *adenosine triphosphate* (ATP) *into cyclic adenosine monophosphate* (c AMP). Injection of PGE1 therefore causes a *rise in intracellular cAMP,* causing a *fall in intracellular calcium,* thereby inducing smooth muscle *relaxation*.

PGE1 therapy is associated with good *efficacy and tolerability* in most forms of ED.

The *adverse events* associated with prostaglandin injection therapy are primarily local effects and include penile pain (15%) and priapism (1%) and, in the longer term, penile scarring (1.7%).

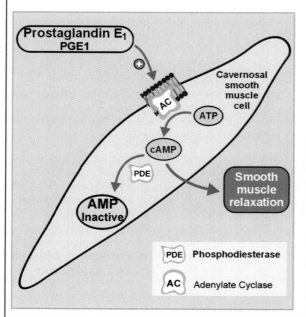

B | Papaverine

Papaverine was the first drug to be used. It is now *rarely used alone,* but mainly in *combination* with PGE1 and/or phentolamine in patients *refractory* to both oral therapy and single-agent injection therapy. Papaverine is a *non-selective* inhibitor of the enzyme *phosphodiesterase* (PDE) in the penis, thereby inhibiting the breakdown of both *cyclic GMP* and *cyclic AMP* resulting in a fall in the cytoplasmic calcium concentration leading to smooth muscle relaxation.

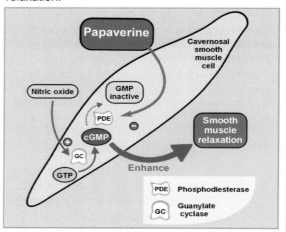

C | Phentolamine

Phentolamine when injected alone has a *modest therapeutic effect.* However, it has a synergistic action when *combined* with drugs such as papaverine or papaverine and PGE1 (as in the case of the trimix). It acts as an *inhibitor* of both *alpha-1 and alpha-2 adrenoceptors* antagonizing the action of noradrenaline on the cell. When injected into the penis, it promotes erection by *blocking the tonic sympathetic neuronal activity* which normally produces smooth muscle contraction.

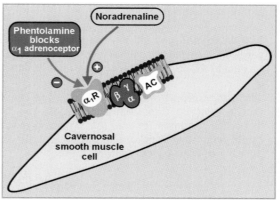

INTRACORPOREAL PHARMACOLOGICAL THERAPY

2 — Local Therapy - Technique of intracorporeal injection

A — Patients must be taught to inject themselves safely and effectively, first in the clinic and later at home

The **technique** is simple and relatively painless. The solution is injected slowly with a **fine needle** into the **side of the shaft** of the penis with the syringe held perpendicular to the skin. The needle is removed and **pressure is applied** to the injection site. The **drug is massaged** gently throughout the shaft of the penis for approximately 30 seconds. Erection **normally** occurs within **5 to 10 minutes.**

Some patients may have **difficulty performing self-injections** because of **poor manual dexterity** or **poor visual acuity. Obesity** can make it difficult for the patient to see his penis, in which case the use of a mirror or injection by the partner may be helpful. **Auto-injectors** can also be helpful. These auto-injectors are similar to those used to inject insulin.

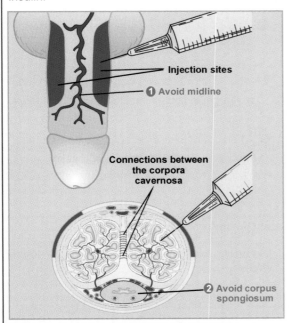

Injection sites
❶ Avoid midline

Connections between the corpora cavernosa

❷ Avoid corpus spongiosum

B — The appropriate dose to be injected must be determined

The initial dose must be **estimated.** The dosage depends on the **etiology of ED. Neurogenic** or **psychogenic** ED can respond to small doses of 2.5 to 5 mcg of PGE1. Patients with **severe vasculogenic** ED may fail to respond to even high doses of single agents. It is usually not worth increasing the dose of

PGE1 **to more than 40 mcg**, but it is preferable to try a **drug combination** with papaverine or phentolamine or both. **25% of patients** who fail to respond to PGE1 alone respond to a combination.

3 — Prolonged Erection

The duration of response of intracavernous injection may be between **50 minutes** and **two** to **three hours.** The patient must be advised that **if erection lasts for more than** about **four hours** he should **promptly seek medical attention**. Treatment with 5 to 10 mg of **terbutaline** orally may abort prolonged erection without the need for further treatment. The risk of prolonged erection is greater with **papaverine** and mixtures containing papaverine than with PGE1 alone. The **management** of prolonged erection after intracavernous injection is described in the chapter "**Priapism**".

4 — Side Effects

SIDE EFFECTS	Pain	Fibrosis	Priapism
	⚡		🕐 > 4 hours
PGE1	15%	1.7%	1%
Bimix	1%	7%	7%
Trimix	5%	7%	10%

Bimix (papaverine + phentolamine)
Trimix (papaverine + phentolamine + PGE1).

Contraindications: Patients at **risk** of **developing priapism** (hematologic disease).
The use of **anticoagulants** is not an absolute contraindication, but extra care must be taken to avoid excessive bruising.

5 — Long-term results

Since the introduction of PDE5-inhibitors, intracorporeal injection is **mainly** used **for patients failing to respond** to **oral therapy.** The **success rate** is about *70%* for PDE1 and *80%* for Trimix. With time, a large proportion of patients **drop out** and **stop treatment.** There are a number of **reasons** for this high drop-out rate, including **ineffective** therapy, patient **dissatisfaction**, partner dissatisfaction, and serious **concomitant** illness. Only one out of three or four patients continues treatment three to four years after starting.

INTRAURETHRAL AND INTRAMEATAL THERAPY

1   Intraurethral therapy

The **urethral mucosa** is **permeable** to drugs. **Alprostadil,** in the form of a **small pellet,** can be administered into the urethra via an administration system called **MUSE** (medicated urethral system for erection). The transfer of active substances to the corpora cavernosa occurs primarily via **venous channels** that communicate between the corpus spongiosum and the corpora cavernosa. MUSE is available in a range of doses of PGE1 from 125 to 1000 mcg. Erection starts within **15 to 30 minutes** and lasts 30 to 60 minutes. The strength of erection can be improved by application of a **constriction ring** in order to reduce proximal absorption.

Although 80% of the drug is absorbed from the urethra within 10 minutes of application, the level of PGE1 in the **ejaculate** could be dangerous in pregnant women, in which case, a **condom** should be used.

A   Efficacy

Efficacy (45% of cases) is inferior to that obtained with PDE5 inhibitors or intracavernosal injection therapy.

C   Advantages and disadvantages

Advantages: no injection required.

Disadvantages: Intolerance due to penile pain and rare dizziness.

Variable efficacy.

B   Administration

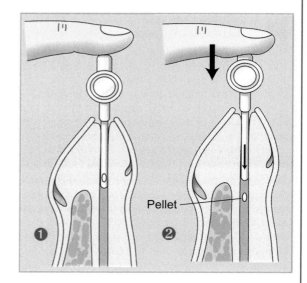

Pellet

❶ The Muse applicator is inserted up to the collar into the meatus

❷ The injector button is pushed down to release the pellet containing PGE1 into the urethra.

❸ The patient then massages the penis to help the distribution of the medication pellet.

2   Intrameatal therapy

Topical (**intrameatal**) application of the combination of **alprostadil** and a dermal **permeation enhancer** is associated with a certain efficacy and tolerability that need to be confirmed by further studies.

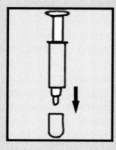  

ANDROGEN REPLACEMENT THERAPY (ART)

1   Definition

Adult-onset **hypogonadism** is a **clinical** and **bio-chemical syndrome** frequently associated with **advancing age** and characterized by a **deficiency in serum androgen levels,** with or without changes in receptor sensitivity to androgens.

It may **affect** the function of **multiple organ systems** and result in significant impairment of **quality of life,** including major alterations of **sexual function.**

2   Clinical diagnosis

In patients with **sexual dysfunction** and at risk of developing or already suspected to suffer from hypogonadism (decreased sexual interest, changes in secondary sexual features), **a testoste-rone** (T) determination with the blood sample taken between 8:00 and 10:00 a.m is **recommended.**

The most accessible and reliable assays to establish the presence of hypogonadism are the measurement of **bio-available T** or **calculated free T** (cFT). Assays for total testosterone, particularly in the elderly, may not reflect the man's true androgenic status.

LABORATORY TESTS
T low
↓
T (confirmation)
LH
FSH
Prolactin

If T levels are below normal or at the lower limit of the accepted normal values, it is wise to **confirm** the results with a second determination together with assessment of **luteinizing hormone** (LH), **follicle stimulating hormone** (FSH) and **prolactin.**

3   Treatment

In men with ED and/or diminished sexual interest, a clear indication (a **clinical picture** together with **biochemical evidence of hypogonadism**) **should exist** prior to initiation of androgen therapy. **Contraindications** should also be ruled out (prostatic or breast cancer, severe bladder neck obstruction).

Testosterone can be given **orally, transdermally** (with patch or gel) or **intramuscularly** (by injection).

Since **androgen replacement therapy** is typically **chronic** or **life-long**, it is essential that all patients receiving androgen therapy be **followed** on a regular basis. The **treating physician** must be **familiar** with the **diagnostic, therapeutic** and **monitoring** aspects of androgen therapy.

1. The patient should be monitored closely for possible **side effects** or **contraindications**, such as abnormal liver function, hyperlipidemia, polycythemia, prostate abnormalities (prostate cancer or severe bladder outlet obstruction), hyperactivity or aggressive behavior, and sleep apnea.

2. **Inadequate** therapeutic **response** or the appearance of significant **adverse effects** call for **reassessment** of treatment indications

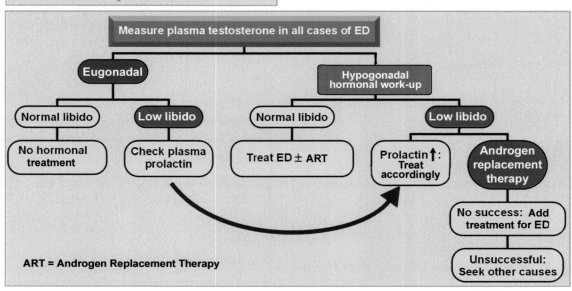

ART = Androgen Replacement Therapy

VACUUM TUMESCENCE DEVICE (VTD)

1 | **A vacuum tumescence device consists of a plastic cylinder, a vacuum pump to produce erection and a constriction ring to maintain erection**

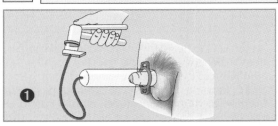

❶ The **cylinder** is placed **over the penis** and held firmly against the pubis to obtain an **airtight seal.**
Suction is then applied to the vacuum pump (manual or battery) to produce a **negative pressure** leading to **engorgement of the penis.**

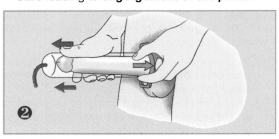

❷ After the *erect state* is achieved a **constriction ring** is slipped from the cylinder onto the base of the penis to **maintain erection.**

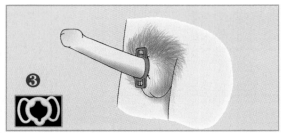

❸ The vacuum is then **released** via a valve and the **cylinder removed.**

Constriction rings may have **various shapes.**

Some have a notch that fits over the urethra to make ejaculation easier.

- **Time taken to achieve erection** is generally, about 2 to 3 minutes.
- The ring should **not be left** on for **more than 30 minutes.**

2 | **Vacuum tumescence devices (VTD) act by developing negative pressure around the penis**

This negative pressure results in a **suction mechanism** that increases blood flow and produces **erection**. This erection is **maintained** by a constricting ring placed around the base of the penis that **decreases venous drainage.**

Hemodynamically, the erection produced by the vacuum device is different from normal erection, as there is **no relaxation** of the trabecular smooth muscle. Blood is sucked into the penis, and the flow is predominantly due to **arterial inflow** and probably also **venous backflow.** Blood mainly accumulates in the intracorporeal spaces of the penis, and also probably between the **corpora and the skin**.

3 | **Contraindications**

- Bleeding conditions.
- Anticoagulant treatment

4 | **Results**

The penis may appear rather **cyanosed** and **cold** and may become painful with time.

VTDs are **effective** to allow intercourse in 70% to 80% of users and the **drop-out rate** at one year is about 60%, which is similar to the drop-out rate for injection treatment. In one study, average use of VTD was **3.5 times per month.**

5 | **Advantages and disadvantages**

DISADVANTAGES	ADVANTAGES
• Cumbersome.	• Noninvasive
• Requires good manual dexterity.	• Effective for all etiologies.
• Coldness of penis. Bruising	
• Ejaculatory block.	

VASCULAR SURGERY

<table>
<tr><td>1</td><td>Objectives: Erection needs a good arterial supply and efficient veno-occlusive mechanism</td></tr>
</table>

The role of vascular surgery in ED is still not well defined. It is only *indicated* in *highly selected* patients and should be performed by *experienced specialists.*

Theoretically, vascular surgery has *3 main objectives:*

1. *Correct penile arterial insufficiency* by revascularization procedures.
2. *Correct venous leakage due* to veno-occlusive dysfunction by reducing venous outflow during erection.
3. Or *both,* as the two pathologies coexist in the majority of cases.

Surgery for ED should only be considered after other treatment possibilities have been exhausted.

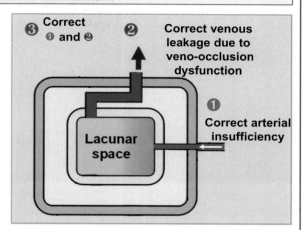

❸ Correct ❶ and ❷

❷ Correct venous leakage due to veno-occlusion dysfunction

❶ Correct arterial insufficiency

Lacunar space

<table>
<tr><td>2</td><td>Surgical technique</td></tr>
</table>

A Arterial revascularization

Who are candidates ?	Technique	Results
• *Young men* <50 years. • History of *trauma* (perineal or penile). • Documented *arterial insufficiency* demonstrated by Doppler and arteriography. • *No other risk factor* for ED.	• Anastomosis between *epigastric artery* and *dorsal penile artery.* 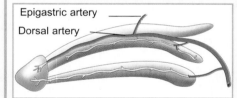 Epigastric artery Dorsal artery	They are *difficult to evaluate* due to the heterogeneous patient populations and inadequate response criteria of the various studies. **Short-term:** about 40% of good results. **Long-term:** about 25% of good results.

B Surgery for veno-occlusion dysfunction ± arterial insufficiency

	Technique	Results
The objective is to *increase* venous outflow *resistance* **Who are candidates ?** • *Proven veno-occlusion incompetence:* **Clinically:** erections for a short period that are difficult to maintain. **Tests:** Doppler ultrasonography and cavernosography reveal veno-occlusion incompetence.	• Dorsal vein arterialization. Anastomosis between *epigastric* artery and *deep dorsal vein* • *Embolization* of penile veins 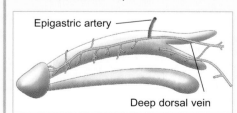 Epigastric artery Deep dorsal vein	Results are *generally poor,* with many series reporting less than 20% of patients capable of spontaneous erections two years after surgery. Results are *better* when selection is limited to *patients* in whom *extensive investigations* establish that a venous leak is the *sole abnormality.*

III.

PENILE PROSTHESES

I   Penile prostheses are the last resort therapy when all other means have failed or are contraindicated.

II   There are two sorts of prostheses: *malleable* devices and *inflatable* devices

1   Malleable prostheses

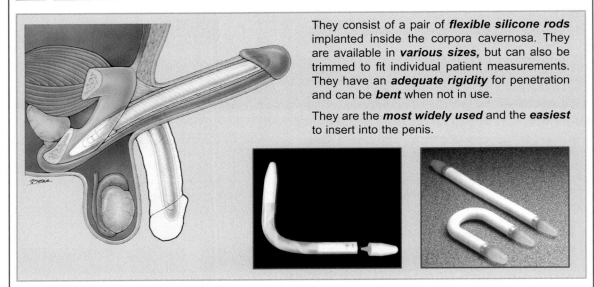

They consist of a pair of *flexible silicone rods* implanted inside the corpora cavernosa. They are available in *various sizes,* but can also be trimmed to fit individual patient measurements. They have an *adequate rigidity* for penetration and can be *bent* when not in use.

They are the *most widely used* and the *easiest* to insert into the penis.

2   Inflatable prostheses

Inflatable penile prostheses are composed of a *pair of penile cylinders,* a *pump* and a *reservoir.* These components can be combined in devices that may consist of *two* or *three* pieces.

A   TWO-PIECE INFLATABLE DEVICES

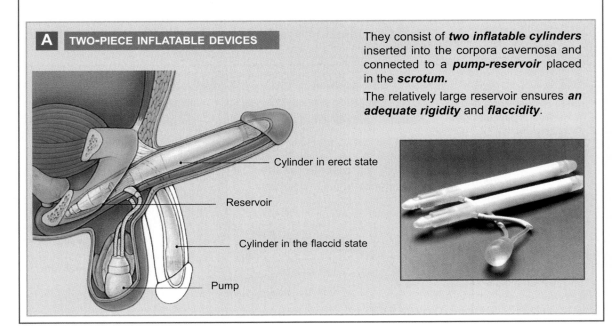

They consist of *two inflatable cylinders* inserted into the corpora cavernosa and connected to a *pump-reservoir* placed in the *scrotum.*

The relatively large reservoir ensures *an adequate rigidity* and *flaccidity*.

Cylinder in erect state

Reservoir

Cylinder in the flaccid state

Pump

PENILE PROSTHESES

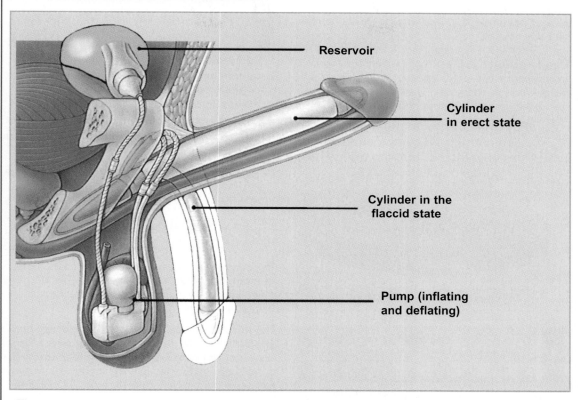

Reservoir

Cylinder
in erect state

Cylinder in the
flaccid state

Pump (inflating
and deflating)

They are **more complex to insert,** but give more satisfactory results. They consist of two completely inflatable **hollow cylinders** connected to a **pump** device placed in the scrotum that can inflate or deflate the prosthesis. The fluid is provided by a **reservoir** placed beneath the rectus abdominis muscles. The volume of the reservoir is significant, allowing **excellent erect and flaccid states** with good cosmetic results during flaccidity.

3 Complications

* *Pain*
* *Infection* (about 1-5%). Higher infection rates are observed in patients with diabetes, autoimmune diseases and prosthesis revision. Infection requires prosthesis removal. **New antibiotic-coated implants** should reduce infection rates.
* *Mechanical failures* are less than 5% in the first year, about 20% at five years and 50% at ten years.

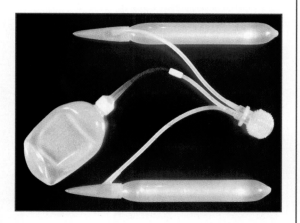

4 Results

Satisfaction rates range from 66% to 92% for patients and 60% to 80% for partners.

III.

PSYCHOSEXUAL AND COUPLE THERAPY

Psychosocial factors play an *important role* in the development of ED. Health professionals who treat men with ED must have a good knowledge of the *role of psychological and interpersonal causes*, and the potential value of psychosexual or couple therapy for ED. Understanding of these factors will lead to more holistic and comprehensive management approaches. Psychosexual therapy may also be of value in addressing *partner issues* and the role of the *couple's relationship.*

1	**Psychosocial factors can be identified alone or in combination with organic factors in more than one half of all cases of ED**

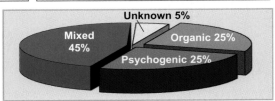

Unknown 5%
Mixed 45%
Organic 25%
Psychogenic 25%

2	**Psychosocial Determinants of Sexual Dysfunction**

A	**Predisposing and Remote Factors.** These are early developmental factors or temperamental traits that predispose individuals to sexual dysfunction

1. Introverted, anxious or antisocial personality
2. Atypical development history, social deprivation
3. Early sexual trauma or abuse
4. Gender identity conflicts
5. Some religious concepts
6. Lack of sexual education

B	**Immediate and Maintaining Factors.** These are factors in the current situation or recent past that precipitate or maintain sexual dysfunction in vulnerable individuals

1. Comorbid anxiety or depression
2. Couple or relationship problems (e.g., couple conflict, partner sexual dysfunction)
3. Performance anxiety (e.g. fear of failure)
4. Loss of sexual attraction or desire
5. Life stresses (e.g., childbirth, infertility, loss of a partner, unemployment)

BOTH IMMEDIATE AND REMOTE CAUSES NEED TO BE ADDRESSED WHEN EVALUATING PSYCHOSOCIAL ASPECTS OF SEXUAL DYSFUNCTION

3	**Indications for Psychosexual Therapy**

Psychosexual therapy may be offered **alone** or in **combination** with medical treatment as **first-line** management for men with ED or other sexual problems.

For this reason, all health-care providers *should be familiar with the basic concepts and principles of psychosexual and couple therapy.* For some patients, brief education, support and reassurance will be sufficient to restore sexual function.

For others, referral for more *specialized* and intensive counseling is necessary. In either case, physicians should *identify* those individuals who may *benefit from psychosexual or couple therapy*, and make appropriate referrals when indicated. If specialized referral is not available, patients should be provided with simple counseling and education as needed. Due to cost factors and lack of resources, *specialized referral* for psychosexual therapy may be limited or unavailable in some settings. However, *all health-care providers can offer* a supportive and positive relationship, basic information and education about sexual function and dysfunction, and encouragement to address key couple and interpersonal issues.

These approaches can be provided either *alone,* or in *combination* with current medical therapies.

PSYCHOSEXUAL AND COUPLE THERAPY (Continued)

<table>
<tr><td>4</td><td>Who should be referred for specialized psychosexual or couple therapy?</td></tr>
</table>

- Patients who present with significant psychosocial, interpersonal or psychiatric problems.

- Patients who decline to use or fail to respond to current medical therapies.

- Partners with significant sexual or psychiatric problems

<table>
<tr><td>5</td><td>Treatment approaches in psychosexual or couple therapy</td></tr>
</table>

With increased awareness of the role of psychosocial factors in sexual dysfunction, a *variety of therapeutic approaches* have been developed. These approaches are based on the early work of **Masters**

and Johnson, who emphasized the importance of the *couple's relationship* and the potentially destructive effects of **performance anxiety ("spectatoring")** on sexual performance. The so-called **"sensate focus"** approach to treatment involves a program of graduated increases in sexual stimulation with instruction to minimize performance demands. Sexual and non-sexual forms of communication are strongly encouraged. Treatment is focused on improving the couple's relationship and reducing anxiety by means of **cognitive** (i.e. educational) and **behavioral** (i.e., learning) methods.

Couples are encouraged to develop a new **"sexual script"**, which is more flexible and pleasure-oriented, and less focused on sexual intercourse and performance. **Improved communication** between patient and therapist, and between the two partners is also strongly encouraged.

With support and guidance from the therapist, the couple are encouraged to undertake a series of activities **("sexual homework")** on a regular basis, usually two to three times per week. The couple is advised to set aside time for these exercises, when they are least likely to be tired or distracted. Couples are typically instructed to **refrain from sexual intercourse** during the early weeks of treatment, and to focus instead on **mutual pleasuring** and **non-demand forms of stimulation**.

The amount and intensity of sexual stimulation are increased gradually, until the couple is able to resume sexual intercourse with minimal tension or anxiety. Strong emphasis is placed throughout on the **direct communication of both sexual and non-sexual needs**.

Psychosexual and couple counseling techniques are highly dependent on **patient and partner motivation**. Accordingly, this approach is usually reserved for **consenting couples**, or individuals with a **high degree of motivation**. Treatment is most likely to be successful in couples with a stable and committed relationship.

III.

6	**TREATMENT OUTCOMES:** **How well does it work?**

The long-term outcome of psychosexual or couple therapy in the treatment of ED has not been adequately investigated. ***Variable rates of efficacy*** have been reported, depending on the selection of patients, duration and intensity of treatment, and types of outcomes assessed.

The high rates of efficacy observed in the early studies by Masters and Johnson have generally ***not been replicated in subsequent studies***. More recent studies have shown variable efficacy rates of 20% to 80%, depending on the following factors:

- Quality of the couple's ***relationship,*** particularly the degree of relationship satisfaction of the partner.

- ***Motivation*** of both partners, particularly the male

- Presence of ***psychiatric illness*** in either partner

- ***Physical attraction*** between the partners

- ***Early compliance*** with the treatment program

7	**Combined medical and** **psychosexual therapy**

Just as sexual problems typically arise from a combination of physical and psychosocial causes, ***medical*** and ***psychosexual treatment*** approaches should be ***combined*** whenever possible. Although ***controlled studies are lacking*** to support the efficacy of combined treatment approaches compared to medical or psychosexual treatments alone, expert opinion strongly favors the use of a ***combined treatment approach*** in most cases. Each of the methods described above can be used alone or in combination with current medical therapies for ED. These approaches are particularly recommended in the following situations:

- Patients who have been sexually inactive for an extended period of time (e.g. several years).

- Patients with comorbid sexual (e.g. premature ejaculation) or psychiatric (e.g. mood) disorders

- Partner sexual dysfunction (e.g., hypoactive sexual desire)

- Significant relationship distress.

Combined treatments need to take into account the level of ***biopsychosocial complexity*** and ***available resources***, and to provide interventions accordingly. There are ***no contraindications*** for the combined use of medical and psychosexual therapies, other than lack of patient motivation or absence of medical or financial resources. A new ***integrated model*** of medical and psychosocial management for sexual dysfunction is strongly advocated. This model reflects the clinical reality in most cases, and aims to provide a more ***patient-centered*** and holistic approach to ***treatment.***

With the advent of oral therapies, clinicians frequently ***neglect*** the role of ***psychological*** or ***couple relationship*** factors in ED. Recent studies indicate that a high rate of ***patient dropout*** or ***dissatisfaction*** with treatment may result when these factors are ***not addressed*** by either primary care clinicians or specialists involved in the treatment of ED.

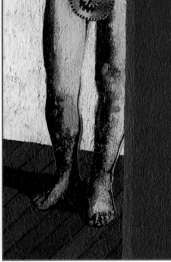

® Poizat

TREATMENT STRATEGY FOR ERECTILE DYSFUNCTION

A *variety of treatment options are* available to the clinician, including *medical, psychological* and *surgical treatments* for ED. Whenever possible, the *choice of therapy* should be based on careful matching of the *patient's needs* and *preferences* with the available *treatment options.* The choice of therapy is strongly *influenced* by personal, cultural, ethnic, religious and economic (affordability) factors. As noted above, assessment of *all patients must include sexual*, *medical* and *psychosocial history, physical examination* and *focused laboratory testing* in conjunction with or prior to initiation of therapy. *Treatment options* should be carefully *reviewed* with the patient and the patient's partner, if available. The *goal of therapy* should be viewed as *restoration of a satisfactory sexual life,* not only a rigid erection.

The *main steps* of the treatment *strategy* are as follows:

I	**Address risk factors and comorbidities**

In parallel to direct treatment for ED, good medical practice recognizes the value of altering *modifiable risk factors.* Although frequently insufficient to reverse ED completely, this step may be of great value in selected patients. Since ED may be a marker of underlying cardiovascular, metabolic or depressive illness, these comorbidities should be addressed whenever possible.

Potentially modifiable risk factors and comorbidities include the following:

1 Lifestyle and psychosocial factors

Lifestyle factors, such as obesity, cigarette smoking, alcoholism or substance abuse may require priority management specific to the particular issue.

Psychosocial factors include relationship issues e.g. partner conflict, mood problems and depression, or other psychosexual dysfunctions.

2 Prescription or non-prescription drug use

Commonly used antihypertensive agents (e.g. diuretics, beta-blockers), psychotropic drugs (e.g. antidepressants, neuroleptics), in addition to antiarrhythmics, antiandrogens and steroids.

Alterations in drug dosages or *classes* may be of significant benefit in selected patients, but this should be *coordinated* with the primary physician wherever possible.

3	**Hormone replacement therapy for hormonal abnormalities (e.g. hypogonadism, hyperprolactinemia)**

In men with ED and/or diminished interest, a *clear indication* (a clinical picture together with biochemical evidence of hypogonadism) should exist prior to initiation of androgen therapy. Since androgen replacement therapy is typically chronic or life-long, all patients receiving androgen therapy must be followed on a regular basis. The treating physician must be *familiar* with the diagnostic, therapeutic and monitoring aspects of *androgen therapy.*

II	**Counsel and educate the patient and partner if available about sexuality**

Lack of knowledge about normal sexual function and age-related changes in men and women and *lack of experience* or ability in normal foreplay or intercourse techniques may contribute to sexual dysfunction.

Sexual counseling and *education* for individuals or couples addresses specific psychological or interpersonal factors such as *relationship distress, sexual performance concerns, dysfunctional communication patterns* and *comorbid sexual conditions* that are likely to impact sexual functioning.

Modified sex therapy may serve as an *adjunct to* the other direct therapies for ED to address psychological reactions to these medical or surgical therapies which may be perceived as temporary, unnatural or unacceptable by the patient and/or partner. The *advantages* of psychosexual therapy include its noninvasive nature and broad applicability.

The *disadvantages* of psychosexual therapy include its variable efficacy in the treatment of ED, cost and acceptability by the patient or the couple and availability of qualified providers. *Psychosexual counseling* should be considered *prior* to or in *conjunction* with medical therapy, whenever indicated.

III.

III — Medical Treatment for ED

The *majority of patients* will need to consider *direct treatment* options for ED

Several issues must be adressed *before* initiation of the direct treatment.

1 Shared decision-making

The development of ED can significantly affect the patient's quality of life, but it is not a life-threatening disease. Consequently, it is reasonable to *discuss the benefits, risks, and costs* of the available treatment strategies with the patient and have the *patient actively participate* in the *choice of therapy.*

2 Cardiovascular safety

An *important issue* prior to the institution of any therapy and the subsequent resumption of sexual activity is the patient's *overall cardiovascular condition. Is this patient able to resume the exercise of sexual activity?* If not, priority cardiovascular assessment and intervention may be appropriate.

3 Partner issues

If possible, the partner's sexual function should be considered prior to initiating therapy.

4 Which drugs for ED treatment?

Only those *pharmacological treatments* that have been thoroughly tested in *randomized clinical trials,* with subsequent publication of results in *peer-reviewed literature,* should be considered for general use.

5 Criteria of selection

The *treatment selected* by a patient will be *influenced* not only by issues such as *efficacy* and *safety,* but also by the patient's *cultural, religious and economic background.*

Additionally, factors such as (1) ease of administration, (2) invasiveness, (3) reversibility, (4) cost, (5) mechanism of action (peripheral vs central, inducer vs enhancer) and (6) legal regulatory approval and availability *may all critically influence* the individual patient's choice of therapy.

6 The use of internet

The use of the internet to prescribe therapies for erectile dysfunction is to be *strongly discouraged* since it fails to meet the need for direct physician-patient contact in the assessment of all patients presenting with this complaint.

IV — Treatment strategy (see algorithm)

V — Reassessment and follow-up

Reassessment and *follow-up* should be conducted at *regular intervals* for all patients receiving treatment for ED. The *goals* of follow-up *include:*

1. The need for *dose titration* or *substitution of another treatment* intervention should be considered at each treatment follow-up visit. Patients may change treatment preferences, seek new information, or wish to re-evaluate their current treatment choices.

2. *Patient communication.* Patients may have concerns regarding treatment administration, other sexual dysfunctions (e.g. premature ejaculation), partner issues (e.g. anorgasmia) or lifestyle factors (e.g. emotional stress).

3. *Patients may change medication regimens,* either for ED or a concomitant medical disorder. The possibility of adverse *drug reactions* or *drug interaction* effects with oral medications for ED should be carefully *monitored.*

4. *General medical and psychosocial reassessment* should occur at *regular intervals,* depending upon the patient's health, physical and psychosocial needs. *Follow-up* also provides an *additional* opportunity for *patient education.*

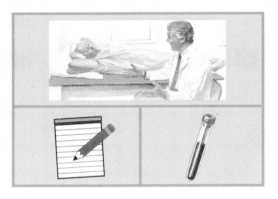

TREATMENT STRATEGY OF ERECTILE DYSFUNCTION (ALGORITHM)

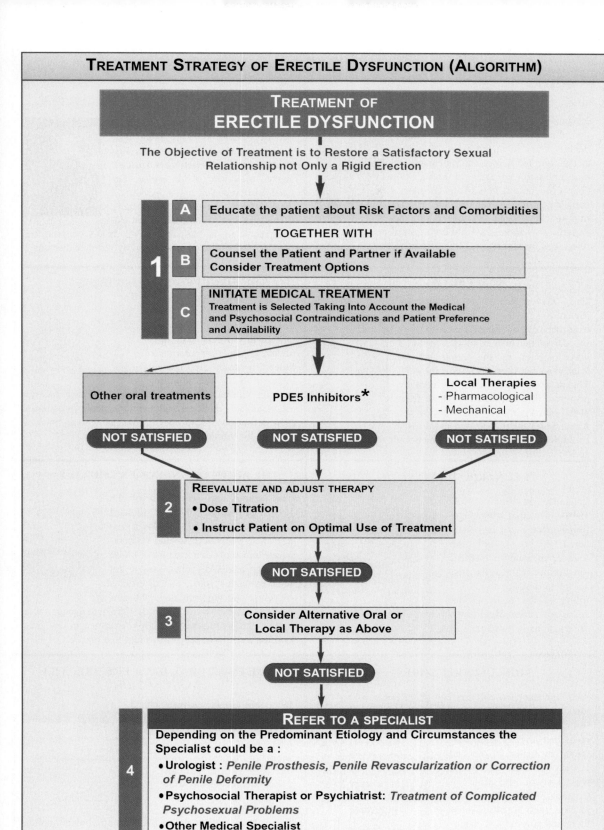

TREATMENT OF ERECTILE DYSFUNCTION

The Objective of Treatment is to Restore a Satisfactory Sexual Relationship not Only a Rigid Erection

1

A Educate the patient about Risk Factors and Comorbidities

TOGETHER WITH

B Counsel the Patient and Partner if Available
Consider Treatment Options

C INITIATE MEDICAL TREATMENT
Treatment is Selected Taking Into Account the Medical and Psychosocial Contraindications and Patient Preference and Availability

Other oral treatments

PDE5 Inhibitors*

Local Therapies
- Pharmacological
- Mechanical

NOT SATISFIED   NOT SATISFIED   NOT SATISFIED

2 REEVALUATE AND ADJUST THERAPY
- Dose Titration
- Instruct Patient on Optimal Use of Treatment

NOT SATISFIED

3 Consider Alternative Oral or Local Therapy as Above

NOT SATISFIED

4 REFER TO A SPECIALIST
Depending on the Predominant Etiology and Circumstances the Specialist could be a :
- Urologist : *Penile Prosthesis, Penile Revascularization or Correction of Penile Deformity*
- Psychosocial Therapist or Psychiatrist: *Treatment of Complicated Psychosexual Problems*
- Other Medical Specialist

***PDE5 inhibitors are the preferred treatment option in the large majority of patients*

III.

ANCIENT MILESTONES IN SEXUAL DYSFUNCTION

PHARAONIC EGYPT

Ithyphallic depictions – like that of the god Min in the Temple of Luxor - are frequently found in ancient Egyptian culture as the erect penis was a sign of good fortune and masculine strength. Prescription 663 of the famous Ebers Papyrus offers a variety of remedies for the cure of male impotence. Other passages of this Papyrus also address several contraceptive recipes for women.

KAMA SUTRA

The *"Kama Sutra"* (Aphorisms on Pleasure) is the earliest surviving example of a comprehensive love manual in the history of the world. It was compiled by the Indian scholar Vatsayana between 330 and 369 A.D. The descriptions of many lovemaking postures (illustrations shown here from 18th century) are only one aspect of the Kama Sutra apart from the many psychological insights into the interactions and scenarios of love

LEONARDO DA VINCI

Leonardo da Vinci (1452-1519) – the great artist of the Renaissance - can be considered to be not only the founder of modern medical illustration, but also the first author to describe the blood filling of the penis as the cause of erection. He drew this conclusion from his own observations in human corpses.

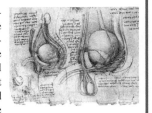

"MUSCULI ERECTORES"

Although the "Musculi erectores penis" (i.e. Mm. bulbospongiosi and ischiocavernosi) had already been described by Galen in the 2nd century A.D., this knowledge was lost at the time of Costanzo Varolio (1543-1575), who re-discovered them and gave an astonishingly correct description of the mechanisms of erection.

PEYRONIE´S DISEASE

Although the "Nodus penis" had been described centuries before, Francois de LaPeyronie (1678-1747) gave the first extended clinical report on the disease named after him in his article *"Sur quelques obstacles qui s'opposent à l'éjaculation naturelle de la semence"* (On some obstacles to the natural ejaculation of the semen) from 1743. In his opinion, the plaque was predominantly caused by venereal diseases.

THE FIRST PENILE PROSTHESIS ?

Paré also suggested an "artificial penis" made of a wooden pipe or tube for patients after traumatic penile amputation in order to facilitate correct micturition in the standing position. Although not intended for sexual activities one might call this device a 16th century "penile prosthesis" as by definition a prosthesis – in contrast with an implant- replaces the whole organ or part of the body.

THE BIRTH OF ANDROGEN THERAPY

The famous self-experiment of the French physiologist Charles Edouard Brown-Séquard (1817-1894) at the age of 72 years with several subcutaneous injections of a mixture of blood from the testicular veins, semen and juice extracted from crushed testicles of young and vigorous dogs and guinea pigs in 1889 was a first milestone of androgen therapy in the aging male although his "pharmaceutical" prescription must have been equivalent to a placebo.

THE FIRST ORAL DRUG FOR ERECTILE DYSFUNCTION

In 1896 the chemist Leopold Spiegel (1865-1927) from Berlin performed chemical characterization of yohimbine from the bark of the African yohimbe tree. He was well aware of the aphrodisiac effect that the bark was said to have in its country of origin and clinical application followed immediately in Europe. Spiegel patented his chemical discovery in the UK in 1900.

II. OTHER DYSFUNCTIONS IN MEN

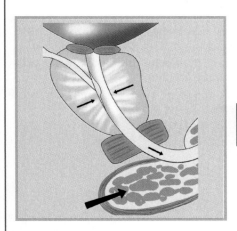

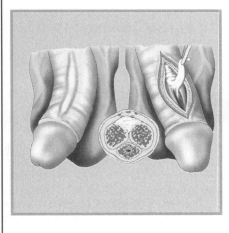

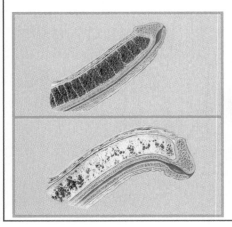

I. EJACULATION AND ORGASMIC DISORDERS

1 | Ejaculate fluid is mainly derived from the seminal vesicles

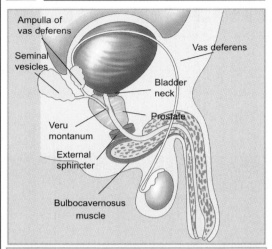

Ampulla of vas deferens
Seminal vesicles
Vas deferens
Bladder neck
Prostate
Veru montanum
External sphincter
Bulbocavernosus muscle

ORIGIN OF THE EJACULATE

Volume:	1,5 – 5 ml
Seminal vesicles	50-70 %
Prostate	15-30 %
Ampulla of vas deferens (contains the sperm)	< 5 %
Periurethral & Cowper's glands small amount	

3 | Neurological control of ejaculation

Emission of seminal fluid and **closure of the bladder neck** are phenomena under **sympathetic control** by thoracolumbar segments T9-L3, while **ejection** of semen is controlled by a **reflex from the pudendal nerve**, which makes both ischiocavernosus and bulbocavernosus muscles **contract**, expelling the **seminal fluid.**

Ejaculation is also **controlled** by the **hypothalamus**, where **dopamine promotes ejaculation** while **serotonin inhibits.**

Orgasm is due to processing of pudendal nerve sensory stimuli by the **brain**.

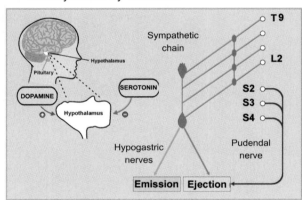

Hypothalamus
Pituitary
DOPAMINE
SEROTONIN
Hypothalamus
Sympathetic chain
T 9
L2
S2
S3
S4
Hypogastric nerves
Pudendal nerve
Emission   Ejection

2 | Ejaculation is divided into two events: Emission and then Ejection of the seminal fluid

A | Emission

The seminal fluid is **excreted forcibly** from the **seminal tract** into the **posterior urethra.** While the **bladder neck closes** and the **external sphincter** remains **closed, pressure builds** up in the dilated **prostatic urethra.**

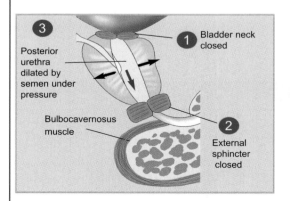

Posterior urethra dilated by semen under pressure
Bulbocavernosus muscle
1 Bladder neck closed
2 External sphincter closed
3

B | Ejection

The **external sphincter opens** while the **bladder neck remains closed** and the **fluid** accumulated in the prostatic urethra is **forcibly ejected** outside from the urethra, helped by **rhythmic contraction** of the perineal muscles including the **bulbocavernosus** muscles that expel the ejaculate.

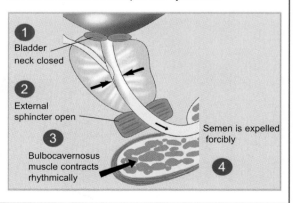

1 Bladder neck closed
2 External sphincter open
3 Bulbocavernosus muscle contracts rhythmically
Semen is expelled forcibly
4

I. EJACULATION AND ORGASMIC DISORDERS

VARIOUS TYPES OF EJACULATORY AND ORGASMIC DISORDERS

DEFINITION	CAUSES
1 Premature Ejaculation (PE) (or early, rapid)  This term implies an inability of the man to **delay** the **time of ejaculation** to his and his partner's **satisfaction.**	This problem is most probably due to **psychosexual** rather than organic problems. Young men tend to ejaculate more rapidly than older men. Premature ejaculation may be due to **a failure to learn** how to delay ejaculation. **Worrying** about this problem makes ejaculation more rapid. The end result may be ejaculation without erection. **Penile hypersensitivity** and a **rapid** ejaculatory **reflex** arc may also be a cause of premature ejaculation. **Orgasm** is due to processing of **pudendal nerve** sensory stimuli by the **brain.** There is a strong **association** between premature ejaculation and **erectile dysfunction**.
2 Delayed Ejaculation and Anejaculation 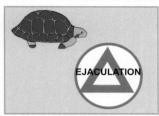 EJACULATION **Delayed ejaculation** is **undue** delay in **reaching a climax** during sexual activity. **Anejaculation** is the **absence of ejaculation** during orgasm.	Failure of ejaculation may occur due to **abnormalities** of **production** or **storage** of semen or conditions affecting the actual **expulsive process. Psychological causes** are common. The patient's history may include **diabetes, neurological disease** or spinal injury. **Surgery** is a common cause of damage to the sympathetic nerve trunks and ejaculatory failure, that may constitute a significant problem, can occur in young men undergoing retroperitoneal lymph node dissection. Lack of seminal fluid following **radical prostatectomy** invariably results in absent ejaculation.
3 Retrograde Ejaculation (RE)  **Retrograde ejaculation** occurs when the **bladder neck fails** to close and all or a large proportion of the ejaculate is **ejected into the bladder.**	The **differential diagnosis** between **anejaculation** and **retrograde ejaculation** can be done easily by assessing the presence of **fructose** and **spermatozoids** in urine after intercourse or masturbation. **Congenital** causes of RE are rare and are due to developmental anomalies of the ejaculatory ducts. **Outflow obstruction** or **iatrogenic** damage to the **bladder neck** following resection of urethral valves or the bladder neck in childhood can lead to RE. The risk is much higher after **bladder neck** or prostate **surgery** in adults (70% to 80% of men). Some **drugs,** such as alpha blockers, can induce RE in 5-15% of cases. **Diabetes** is also a cause of RE (by inducing peripheral neuropathy).
4 Anorgasmia and Orgasmic Dysfunction ORGASM This implies the **inability** to achieve an orgasm, or a markedly **diminished intensity** of orgasmic sensation during conscious sexual activity with or without ejaculation.	It is rare and is most certainly due to **psychological disturbances,** but may also have a **neurogenic cause.**
5 Painful Ejaculation  **Pain** can occur during or **shortly after** ejaculation and may persist for several hours.	Painful ejaculation is usually a symptom of **inflammation** of the **prostate, seminal vesicles or urethra** and should be investigated and treated accordingly.

MANAGEMENT OF PREMATURE EJACULATION (PE)

PATIENT COMPLAINING OF PREMATURE EJACULATION (PE)

PATIENT/PARTNER HISTORY

- Establish presenting complaint
- Intravaginal Ejaculatory Latency Time
- Perceived degree of ejaculatory control
- Degree of patient/partner distress
- Onset and duration of PE
- Psychosocial history
- Medical history
- Physical Examination

PE SECONDARY TO ED OR OTHER SEXUAL DYSFUNCTION

YES → **MANAGE PRIMARY CAUSE**

NO

Counsel the patient and discuss treatment options and patient's preference

TREATMENT

BEHAVIORAL THERAPY
- Stop/Start
- Squeeze Technique
- Sensate Focus

RELATIONSHIP COUNSELING

PHARMACOTHERAPY
- SSRI agents*
- Topical anesthetics

OR

Combination Treatment

ATTEMPT GRADUATED WITHDRAWAL OF PHARMACOTHERAPY AFTER 6 to 8 weeks

---

*Selective serotonin uptake inhibitors (SSRIs)

Paroxetine, sertraline, fluoxetine

Administration :
- Daily treatment
- On demand treatment

- Low daily doses + as needed higher dose shortly before intercourse.

Side effects: fatigue, yawning, mild nausea, perspiration (gradually disappear over 2-3 weeks)

Withdrawal should be gradual (2-3 weeks).

MANAGEMENT OF DELAYED EJACULATION, ANEJACULATION AND ANORGASMIA

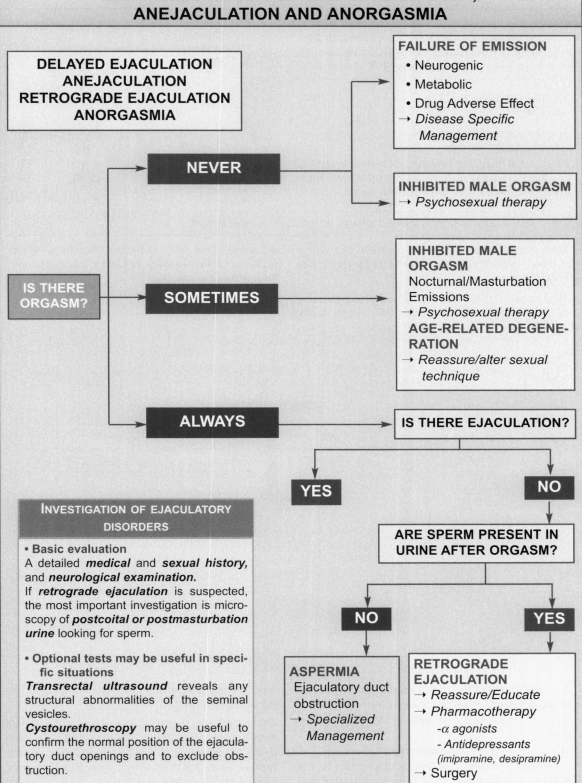

**DELAYED EJACULATION
ANEJACULATION
RETROGRADE EJACULATION
ANORGASMIA**

IS THERE ORGASM?

NEVER

FAILURE OF EMISSION
- Neurogenic
- Metabolic
- Drug Adverse Effect
→ *Disease Specific Management*

INHIBITED MALE ORGASM
→ *Psychosexual therapy*

SOMETIMES

INHIBITED MALE ORGASM
Nocturnal/Masturbation Emissions
→ *Psychosexual therapy*
AGE-RELATED DEGENE-RATION
→ *Reassure/alter sexual technique*

ALWAYS

IS THERE EJACULATION?

YES

NO

ARE SPERM PRESENT IN URINE AFTER ORGASM?

NO

YES

ASPERMIA
Ejaculatory duct obstruction
→ *Specialized Management*

RETROGRADE EJACULATION
→ *Reassure/Educate*
→ *Pharmacotherapy*
  -α agonists
  - Antidepressants
    (imipramine, desipramine)
→ Surgery

INVESTIGATION OF EJACULATORY DISORDERS

- Basic evaluation
A detailed **medical** and **sexual history,** and **neurological examination.**
If **retrograde ejaculation** is suspected, the most important investigation is microscopy of **postcoital or postmasturbation urine** looking for sperm.

- Optional tests may be useful in specific situations
Transrectal ultrasound reveals any structural abnormalities of the seminal vesicles.
Cystourethroscopy may be useful to confirm the normal position of the ejaculatory duct openings and to exclude obstruction.

I.

II. PEYRONIE'S DISEASE

1	**Peyronie's disease is characterized by the formation of a fibrous nodule in the tunica albuginea.**

The prevalence is about 0.4 to 3.5% in men 40-70 years old.

NATURAL HISTORY

The natural history is **variable.** Schematically, 50% of patients **remain stable** after the initial evaluation, 10-20% **improve** and 30-40% **deteriorate.**

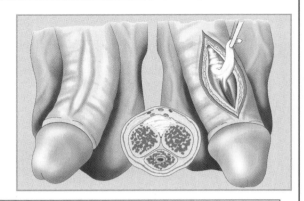

2	**Etiology and pathophysiology are poorly understood.**

Many **possible** etiological factors have been suggested. **Penile trauma** appears to be the most likely factor.

Microtrauma to the penis leads to a **small amount of bleeding** and **fibrin disposition** in the tunica albuginea. This fibrin activates fibroblasts which cause an **inflammatory reaction** leading to the **formation of a plaque.**

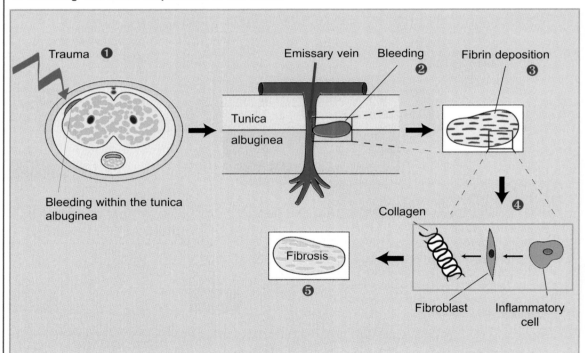

A **minor injury** of the tunica albuginea may rupture an emissary vein and **cause bleeding** within the densely packed sublayers of the **tunica albuginea.**

The ensuing **fibrin deposition** and accumulation of **inflammatory cells** may cause obstruction of the draining veins and resulting in a trapped inflammatory process. This stimulates the fibroblasts to produce **collagen fibers.**

The **elastases** produced can destroy the elastic fiber network and **impair the elasticity.** Together these processes lead to **fibrosis** and produce the **typical symptoms** of Peyronie's disease: **pain, plaque** and **deformity.**

II. PEYRONIE'S DISEASE

<table>
<tr><td>**3**</td><td>**Diagnosis is based on *clinical history* and *physical examination***</td></tr>
</table>

Diagnosis and assessment are summarized in the decision tree. A patient who presents with a "***lump***" in the penis should be **reassured** that he does not have a malignant disease. The doctor should also explain the **natural history** of the disease and the possibility of **spontaneous improvement** or **stabilization** of the disease and **discuss** the **treatment modalities,** their results and their complications.

<table>
<tr><td>**4**</td><td>**Treatment: should be as conservative as possible. Surgery is the last resort**</td></tr>
</table>

Many **oral drugs** have been proposed, but none seems to give better results than Vitamin E ± colchicine. However, these **results** remain limited.

Intralesional injection of corticosteroid and verapamil has been **disappointing.**

Surgery is the last resort treatment.

Before proposing surgery, a number of **important prerequisites** must be present, as summarized in the table.

CONSERVATIVE TREATMENT

Oral Treatment 	Vitamin E ± colchicine has an action on pain. Modest results on plaque and deformity.
Intralesional Injection	Corticosteroids, verapamil. Disappointing results.

PREREQUISITES FOR SURGERY

- Disease **present** for at least **12 months, stable** for at least **6 months**
- Deformity makes **intercourse difficult**
- **Quality of erection** will determine the technique: reconstruction or prosthesis
- **Patient** should be **fully informed** about the outcome and consequences of surgery and must sign a consent agreement.

SURGICAL TREATMENT

1. Plaque *excisions and grafting*	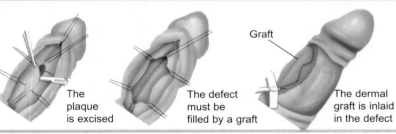 The plaque is excised · The defect must be filled by a graft · Graft · The dermal graft is inlaid in the defect
2. Tunical incision and grafting with saphenous vein or other (to avoid complications of excision of the plaque)	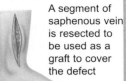 H-shaped transverse relaxing incision in the center of the plaque · The tunical defect is measured by stretching the penis · A segment of saphenous vein is resected to be used as a graft to cover the defect
3. Corporoplasty (plaque is left in place) ❶ Wedge resection ❷ Plication procedures	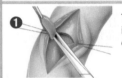 The tunica albuginea is excised on the side opposite to the plaque · The edges are approximated and the penis is straight.
4. Penile prosthesis	❷ Straightening of penis with plication sutures on both sides of the tunica albuginea opposite the plaque

II.

PEYRONIE'S DISEASE MANAGEMENT

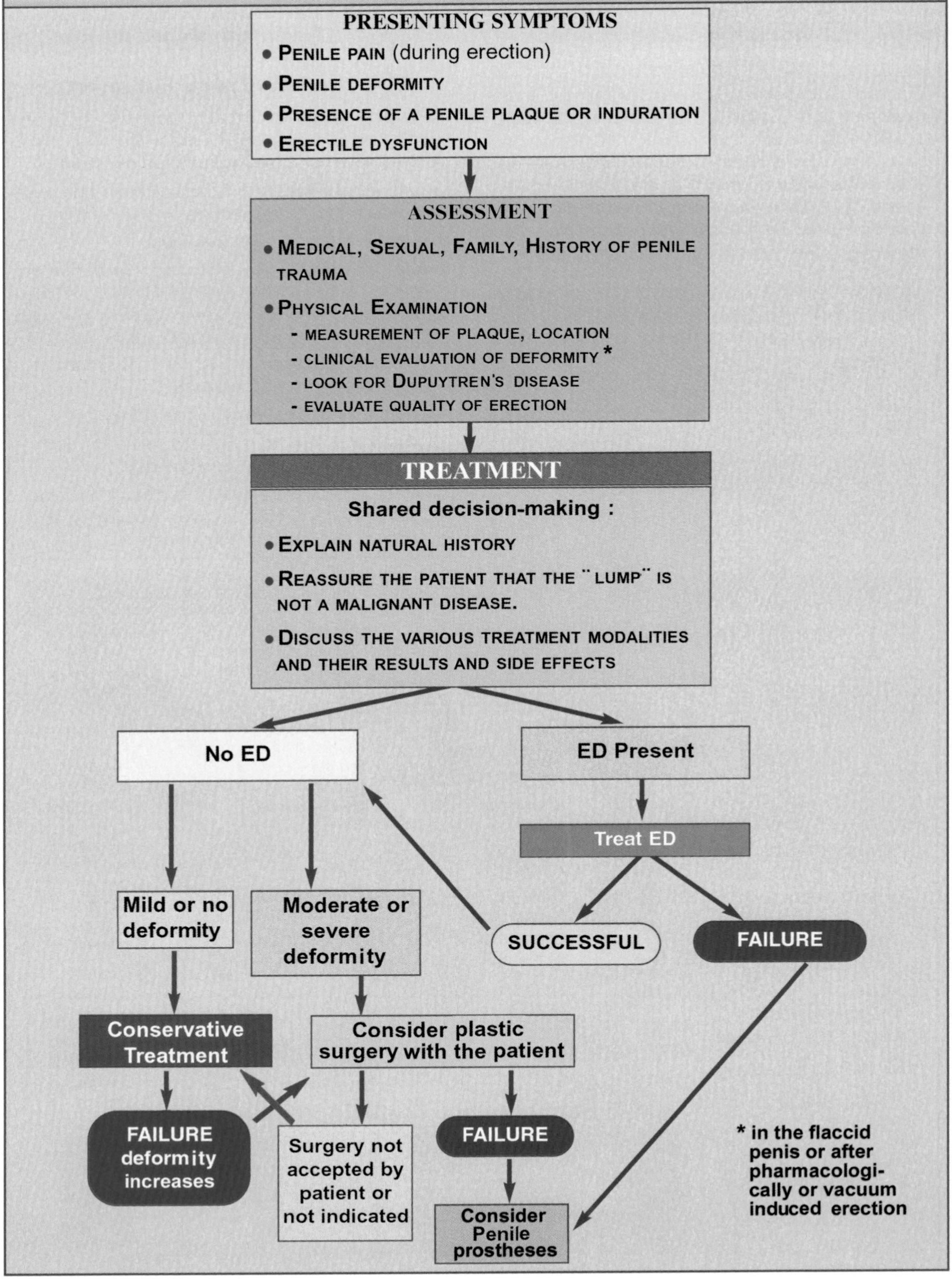

PRESENTING SYMPTOMS
- PENILE PAIN (during erection)
- PENILE DEFORMITY
- PRESENCE OF A PENILE PLAQUE OR INDURATION
- ERECTILE DYSFUNCTION

ASSESSMENT
- MEDICAL, SEXUAL, FAMILY, HISTORY OF PENILE TRAUMA
- PHYSICAL EXAMINATION
  - MEASUREMENT OF PLAQUE, LOCATION
  - CLINICAL EVALUATION OF DEFORMITY *
  - LOOK FOR DUPUYTREN'S DISEASE
  - EVALUATE QUALITY OF ERECTION

TREATMENT

Shared decision-making :
- EXPLAIN NATURAL HISTORY
- REASSURE THE PATIENT THAT THE ¨LUMP¨ IS NOT A MALIGNANT DISEASE.
- DISCUSS THE VARIOUS TREATMENT MODALITIES AND THEIR RESULTS AND SIDE EFFECTS

No ED

ED Present

Treat ED

Mild or no deformity

Moderate or severe deformity

SUCCESSFUL

FAILURE

Conservative Treatment

Consider plastic surgery with the patient

FAILURE deformity increases

Surgery not accepted by patient or not indicated

FAILURE

Consider Penile prostheses

* in the flaccid penis or after pharmacologically or vacuum induced erection

III. PRIAPISM

Definition

Priapism is defined as **unwanted erection not associated** with **sexual desire** or **stimulation**.

Two different types of priapism can be distinguished.

1 — Ischemic (no flow)

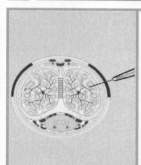

A — MECHANISM

Ischemic priapism or **Low flow** (no flow) is the commonest form. It is due to sudden reduction or **loss** of the normal venous outflow from the penis, leading to failure of detumescence, increasing **anoxia** of the tissues and ultimately necrosis and **fibrosis**. This **condition requires urgent treatment**.

B — ETIOLOGY. THE COMMONEST CAUSE IS IATROGENIC

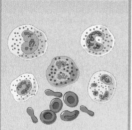

The commonest cause is **iatrogenic**. It is associated with drugs, mainly therapeutic intracavernosal injections, and also sometimes psychotropic drugs, antihypertensives, and anticoagulants. They act by **impairing contraction** of trabecular smooth muscle.

Hypercoagulability syndromes secondary to hematologic conditions, such as sickle cell anemia, multiple myeloma, leukemia, and thalassemia. These conditions **increase sludging** of blood in the cavernosal sinusoids.

2 — High Flow

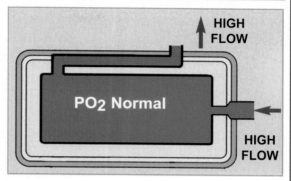

A — MECHANISM

High flow well oxygenated priapism due to **abnormally high arterial blood flow** into the penis. This is much less common than the first type.

B — ETIOLOGY

It is generally secondary to **blunt trauma** of the penis or perineum. Regardless of the cause, a **fistula forms** between the **high pressure** arterial system and the **low pressure** cavernosal sinusoids. This fistula can be demonstrated by color duplex ultrasound or selective penile arteriography.

As there is **no ischemia,** this high flow priapism can persist for several days or even weeks with no permanent changes in the corpora.

3 — Diagnosis

LOW FLOW	HIGH FLOW
• Fully rigid erection	• Semi-rigid erection
• Painfull	• No pain
• Multiple causes mainly intracorporeal injection	• History of trauma (penis, perineum)
• Doppler: no flow	• Doppler: high flow
• Aspiration: dark blood	• Aspiration: red blood

III.

III. PRIAPISM

4   Pathophysiological changes in low flow priapism

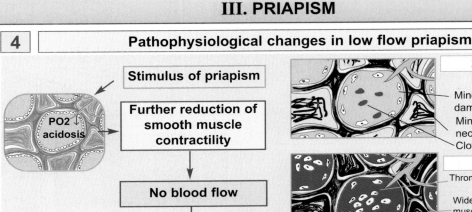

Stimulus of priapism

$PO_2 \downarrow$ acidosis

Further reduction of smooth muscle contractility

No blood flow

HISTOLOGICAL CHANGES

24 hours
- Minor endothelial damage
- Minor smooth muscle necrosis is present
- Clots may form

48 hours
Thrombosis is present

Widespread smooth muscle necrosis
Endothelium destroyed

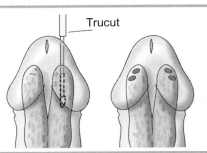

Over 48 hours
- Thrombosis
- Muscle necrosis
- Fibrosis

Long term
Fibrosis

By 12 hours
Minimal endothelial damage

Interstitial edema

5   Treatment   A   MEDICAL (SEE ALGORITHM)

B   SURGICAL TECHNIQUES

Objective: shunting of cavernosal blood to a **low pressure** vascular system (corpus spongiosum or saphenous vein)

❶ Winter technique.
The Trucut needle creates a **communication** between the **cavernosal tissue** and the **spongiosal tissue** of the glans penis

Trucut

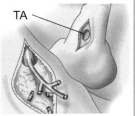

❷ Corporo-spongiosal shunt: direct anastomosis between the corpora cavernosa (CC) and corpus spongiosum (CS)

CC   CS

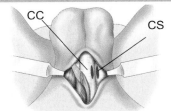

❸ Corporo-saphenous shunt. Saphenous vein (SV) is mobilized and tunneled subcutaneously and anastomosed to the tunica albuginea (TA) of the same side.

TA

SV

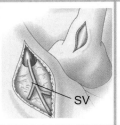
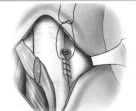
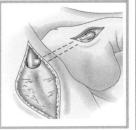

MANAGEMENT OF PRIAPISM

INITIAL MANAGEMENT

- HISTORY
- CLINICAL EXAMINATION
- HEMATOLOGY
- DOPPLER IF EASILY AVAILABLE

↓

FIRST AID MEASURES

- ANALGESIA
- PHYSICAL METHODS
- ORAL DRUGS TO CONTROL ERECTION (terbutaline 5-10 mg)

FAILURE

↓

DEFINITIVE MANAGEMENT

- ASPIRATION Insert an 18 to 20 gauge butterfly needle through the glans to the corpus cavernosum and milk the penis to evacuate old blood
  Apply manual pressure to the penis for several minutes

Black blood → **ISCHEMIC LOW FLOW**

FAILURE

↓

Aspirate another 50 ml of blood
Inject α agonist intracavernosally*

FAILURE

↓

Biopsy + shunt surgery

\+

Rehabilitation

FAILURE

↓

Discuss penile prostheses

ISCHEMIC LOW FLOW → LATE PRESENTATION → Discuss penile prostheses

Normal red blood → **HIGH FLOW NON ISCHEMIC**

↓

Expectant
Compression
Embolization
(surgery)

* Inject 200 to 500 mcg of diluted phenylephrine into the corpus cavernosum every 3-5 minutes until detumescence occurs or until 10 mg total is reached. In older patients, blood pressure and pulse should be monitored.

ERECTILE DISORDERS AND PSYCHOANALYSIS

With the discovery and development of psychoanalysis as an important psychotherapeutic school, Sigmund Freud (1856-1939) from Vienna had a major influence on sexual medicine. The essay with the remarkable title *"Über die allgemeinste Erniedrigung des Liebeslebens"* (The most prevalent form of degradation in erotic life) was published in 1912 and is one of the few publications in which Freud deals directly with male erection disorders.

THE KINSEY REPORT

The biologist Alfred Charles Kinsey (1894-1956) from Bloomington, Indiana, performed the first epidemiologic study on human sexuality by collecting sexual histories from a large number of men and women, resulting in a final sample of about 18,000. The two volumes *"Sexual Behavior in the Human Male"* (1948) and *"Sexual Behavior in the Human Female"* (1953) are milestones in the literature on the anatomy, physiology and psychology of human sexuality.

ERECTILE DYSFUNCTION DUE TO ARTERIAL VASCULAR OCCLUSION

In 1948, the French surgeon René Leriche (1879-1955) first described arterial vascular impotence in thrombotic obliteration of the aortic bifurcation, a syndrome he had already described in detail in the 1920s and which today is named after him. Several strategies were subsequently described to save or reconstruct the internal iliac artery during abdomino-pelvic vascular surgery to maintain or restore erectile function.

THE BIOCHEMICAL BASIS OF PDE-5-INHIBITORS

With his biochemical research, as outlined in the paper *"Fractionation and characterization of a cyclic adenine ribonucleotide formed by tissue"* from 1958, the American Earl W. Sutherland (1915-1974) discovered the physiological significance of cyclic nucleotides in the regulation of cell and tissue function. This basic knowledge – for which he was awarded the Nobel Prize in Medicine and Physiology in 1971 – was also fundamental for the understanding of the first effective oral treatment of ED at the end of the 20th century.

WILLIAM H. MASTERS AND VIRGINIA E. JOHNSON: PRACTICAL SEX-THERAPY

"There is no such entity as an uninvolved partner in a marriage contending with any form of sexual inadequacy." The therapeutic approaches used by Masters and Johnson are oriented towards therapy of the "marital-unit", i.e. the couple, with a strong component of exercising, rather than focussing on verbal aspects of therapy. "Human Sexual Inadequacy" from 1970 is one of their milestone publications.

MICROSURGICAL REVASCULARIZATION OF THE PENIS

In 1973 Václav Michal from Prague reported the first microsurgical treatment of vascular ED by performing a direct anastomosis of the inferior epigastric artery to the corpus cavernosum. In the 1980s further techniques were introduced by Michal himself, as well as by Ronald Virag from Paris and Dieter Hauri from Zurich.

INFLATABLE PENILE IMPLANTS

The breakthrough in penile implant surgery was initiated by F. Brantley Scott from Houston, Texas, together with his colleagues William E. Bradley and Gerald W. Timm when they implanted the first silicone inflatable device on February 2nd, 1973.

INTRACAVERNOUS INJECTION THERAPY FOR ERECTILE DYSFUNCTION

The French vascular surgeon Ronald Virag from Paris discovered the proerectile effect of the vasoactive drug papaverine when injected into the corpus cavernosum in 1982. The injection of phenoxybenzamine was suggested by Giles S. Brindley from London the following year and Adrian W. Zorgniotti from New York introduced drug combination of papaverine and phentolamine in 1985